Printing as an Art

BY

RAY NASH

A HISTORY OF THE SOCIETY OF PRINTERS

1905 · BOSTON · 1955

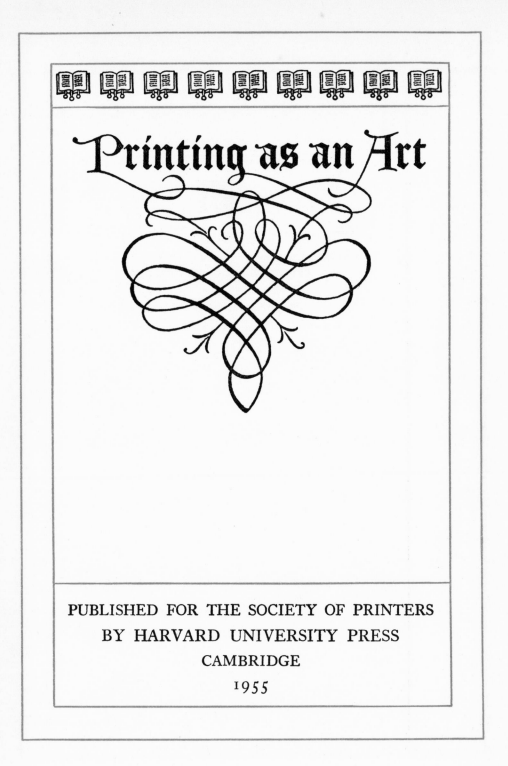

Printing as an Art

PUBLISHED FOR THE SOCIETY OF PRINTERS
BY HARVARD UNIVERSITY PRESS
CAMBRIDGE
1955

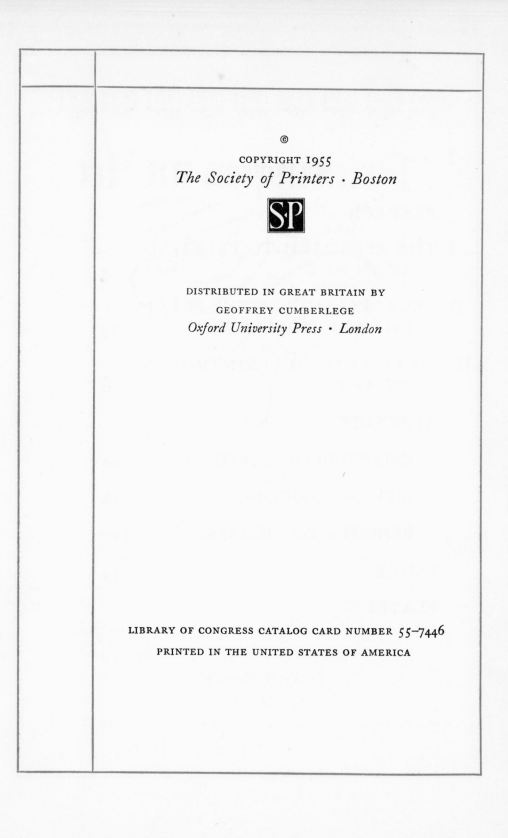

Contents

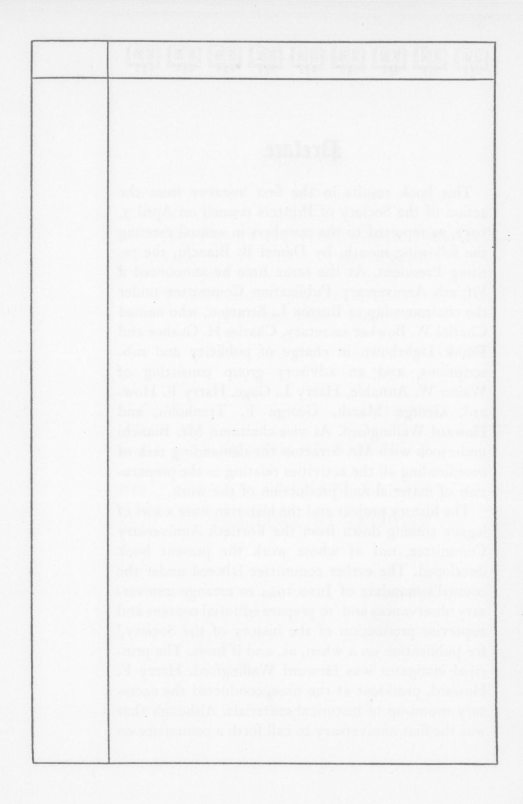

Preface

This book results in the first instance from the action of the Society of Printers council on April 3, 1952, as reported to the members in annual meeting the following month, by Daniel B. Bianchi, the retiring President. At the same time he announced a Fiftieth Anniversary Publication Committee under the chairmanship of Burton L. Stratton, who named Charles W. Bowker secretary, Charles H. Gushee and Frank Lightbown in charge of publicity and subscriptions, and an advisory group consisting of Walter W. Annable, Harry L. Gage, Harry F. Howard, George Marsh, George F. Trenholm, and Howard Wallingford. As vice-chairman Mr. Bianchi undertook with Mr. Stratton the demanding task of coordinating all the activities relating to the preparation of material and production of the work.

The history project and the historian were a sort of legacy coming down from the Fortieth Anniversary Committee, out of whose work the present book developed. The earlier committee labored under the council's mandate of June 1944 to arrange anniversary observances and 'to prepare editorial content and supervise production of the history of the Society,' for publication on a when, as, and if basis. The principal instigator was Howard Wallingford. Harry F. Howard, president at the time, conducted the necessary round-up of historical materials. Although that was the first anniversary to call forth a committee on the Society's history, five years earlier still George F. Trenholm as president had brought up the subject forcefully in a meeting which produced a suggestion that the Society publish an historical account of itself on its fiftieth birthday 'or prior dissolution.'

All those mentioned so far — and many others who must go unnamed because of space limitations — have made substantial contributions to the enterprise. None has been more generous than Bruce Rogers, whose acceptance of the role of designer assured the book distinction from the outset.

If the history succeeds in throwing any new light on the period, place, and people it is engaged with, the credit is largely due to friendly help in supplying the chronicler with out-of-the-way materials bearing upon the story. Of those who helped, several have died during the past decade. I am especially indebted to Mrs. Mabel Wood Johnson, widow of Henry Lewis Johnson, the prime mover, for much personal data regarding him and his associations. Also I have to express gratitude for generous help to John Bianchi, C. Chester Lane, Edward K. Robinson, and Carl Purington Rollins, and to the late Walt Harris, William Dana Orcutt, and Herbert G. Porter. Clarence E. Sherman kindly arranged to let me borrow the pertinent material from the D. B. Updike collection under his charge in the Providence Public Library. The book has benefited in clarity and sense from the attentions of Miss Eleanor Bates as copy editor. She also prepared the index. E. Harold Hugo, who supervised the making of the reproductions, in effect performed also the service of joint editor of illustrations, for all of which he has my thanks.

To the several firms named elsewhere, I join in expressing grateful acknowledgment of generous treatment with respect to goods and services which have made the publication possible.

R. N.

Hanover, New Hampshire
21 December 1954

Printing as an Art

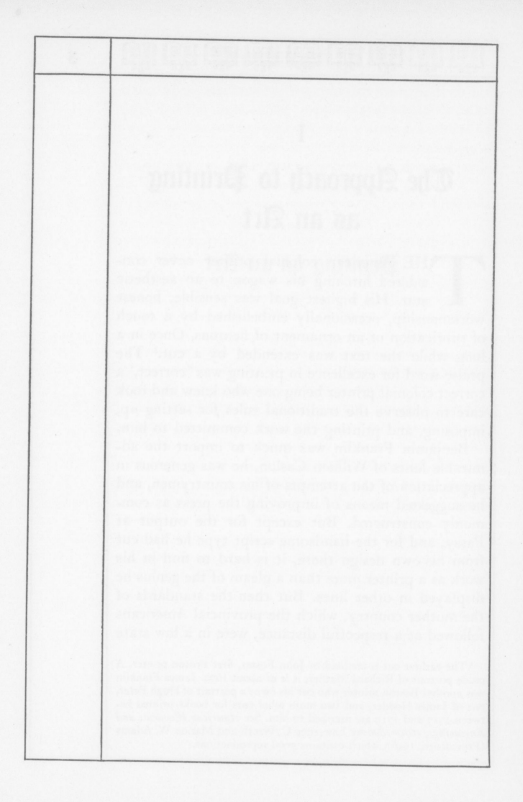

I

The Approach to Printing as an Art

THE American colonial printer never considered hitching his wagon to an aesthetic star. His highest goal was sensible, honest workmanship, occasionally embellished by a touch of rubrication or an ornament of fleurons. Once in a long while the text was extended by a cut.[1] The praise-word for excellence in printing was 'correct,' a correct colonial printer being one who knew and took care to observe the traditional rules for setting up, imposing, and printing the work committed to him.

Benjamin Franklin was quick to import the admirable fonts of William Caslon, he was generous in appreciation of the attempts of his countrymen, and he suggested means of improving the press as commonly constructed. But except for the output at Passy, and for the handsome script type he had cut from his own design there, it is hard to find in his work as a printer more than a gleam of the genius he displayed in other lines. But then the standards of the mother country, which the provincial Americans followed at a respectful distance, were in a low state

---

[1] The earliest cut is credited to John Foster, first Boston printer. A crude portrait of Richard Mather, it is of about 1670. James Franklin was another Boston printer who cut his own: a portrait of Hugh Peter, one of James Hodder, and two more relief cuts for books printed between 1717 and 1719 are ascribed to him. See *American Woodcuts and Engravings, 1670–1800* by Lawrence C. Wroth and Marion W. Adams (Providence, 1946), which contains good reproductions.

when John Baskerville brought his wealth, enthusiasm, and the taste of the 'copperplate' writing master to the reform of typography. Only after his efforts in the amateur spirit and only in the British homelands did printers of the eighteenth century begin to speak of 'beauty of workmanship.'

Franklin's younger contemporary, Isaiah Thomas, is a likelier candidate for the place of earliest American fine printer. He possessed great energy, and ambition to excel, along with the historical sense of one who assisted at a successful revolution of government as well as of his trade. His proudest achievement in bookmaking was Charlotte Smith's *Elegiac Sonnets* which he printed on the first native wove paper, from his own mill at Worcester, in 1795. But it does not seriously rival the Birmingham printer's standards of design and workmanship.[2]

The most successful early attempt of American printers to answer the challenge from overseas was probably *The Columbiad* (Philadelphia, 1807) by

[2] Following Baskerville, English fine printing advanced notably at the Shakespeare Press, London, from which William Bulmer wrote in the advertisement to *Poems by Goldsmith and Parnell*, 1795: 'To raise the Art of Printing in this country from the neglected state . . . much has been done within the last few years; and the warm emulation . . . amongst the Printers of the present day . . . has been highly patronized by the public in general. The present volume, in addition to the . . . many other valuable works of elegance, which have already been given to the world . . . are particularly meant to combine the various beauties of PRINTING, TYPE-FOUNDING, ENGRAVING, and PAPER-MAKING; as well with a view to ascertain the near approach to perfection which those arts have attained in this country, as to invite a fair competition with the best Typographical Productions of other nations. . . .' He goes on to give William Martin credit for the types and Thomas Bewick and associates for the wood-engravings.

Fine printing made its appearance as a recognized department in *The Printer's Grammar* (London, 1808), by Caleb Stower. The author of the particular article was John McCreery, a Liverpool printer whose poetic *The Press*, published five years earlier, is itself a typographical piece. At least one copy of Stower came promptly to Boston and was acquired the year after publication by Samuel T. Armstrong, of Charlestown.

Joel Barlow, one of the Hartford Wits. This luxurious quarto was printed by Fry & Kammerer of Philadelphia from types supplied by the foundry then recently established by Binny & Ronaldson. If its heroic couplets are no longer widely read (the author had some reputation in Europe as well as in his own country), the volume is still sought as an example of fine printing and is honored in the name of the Columbiad Club of bookmen in Connecticut.

Until the nineteenth century printers regarded themselves as men of letters. Their energies and ambitions were more likely to be spent in writing for the press than in making handsome arrangements and 'neat' (for so the praise-word had become) impressions of its product. The best among them had been drawn to the trade through bookish propensities or fascination with scribbling. The idea that a self-respecting printer would of course edit his own newspaper or magazine, just as he expected to correct the orthography of 'copy' turned in by statesmen and savants, was first challenged at the turn of the century. By mid-century the species printer-editor was practically extinct.[3]

The explanation of how and why the early printer, from regarding himself as a man of letters, by degrees came to think of his calling primarily as that of a man of business, is complicated by many more factors than can be looked into here. However, it may be recalled that the social effects in revolutionary eighteenth-century America were more profoundly

[3] In 1848 Joseph Tinker Buckingham believed he was the only remaining printer who edited his own paper in Boston if not in the Commonwealth. He recalled that in 1801 (misprinted 1811) the *Palladium* made a fresh start in charge of a professional editor, the earliest of his kind. See Buckingham's remarks in *Proceedings at the Printers' Festival . . . Franklin Typographical Society . . . January 15, 1848* (Boston, 1848); also his *Specimens of Newspaper Literature* (Boston, 1850), II, 160.

moving than was realized, or even intended, by the Boston radicals who were changing the government. Toward the end of the century and through the early years of the nineteenth there was an accelerated shifting, accompanied frequently by jolts, in the process of adjusting to the changing structure. Isaiah Thomas, the old revolutionist, need not have been surprised when his partner wrote him from Boston that 'the devil seems to have got into the journeymen,' who were making new wage demands. All this was expressed in various new organizations.

The earliest printers' association, the Society of Printers of Boston and Vicinity, was formed by the employing printers of New England in 1805.[4] In 1808 its name was changed to the Faustus Association. The principal purpose of the organization was to fix prices to be charged for the members' products and to reach agreement on 'certain rules to be observed in relation to apprentices and journeymen.' In the main the members' concerns were limited to those of prudent tradesmen, but some interest in the direction of better printing is reflected in their efforts to improve the quality of native paper and to bring about the adoption of patent leather ink-balls as superior to the ordinary kind. They conducted an investigation into the comparative merits of American and imported printing types but their judgments of

[4] The historian of the Society was its last surviving member, Joseph T. Buckingham, who in the Boston *Evening Transcript* in September 1859 published a series of articles based on the manuscript record book of the association. This 'Constitution and Records of the Society of Printers of Boston and Vicinity' was turned up in a garret and presented earlier that year to Buckingham, who passed it on to the Franklin Typographical Society. There Charles L. Nichols saw it, as reported in the *Bulletin of the American Antiquarian Society*, No. 3, May 19, 1914. Since then the manuscript has disappeared, presumably destroyed by the fire which consumed the Franklin Typographical Society documents.

quality were entirely on the basis of durability rather than design. The annual dinner was an occasion for oratory in the magniloquent fashion of the time, for odes and toasts.[5] This early prototype of the Typothetae dissolved in 1815.

As early as 1795 another association had been established which included printers among its members and which had its part to play in the chronicle of printing as an art. This was the long-lived Massachusetts Charitable Mechanic Association, with membership open to the right-living master mechanic and manufacturer (defined as 'a proprietor of a manufactory, or a superintendent thereof').[6] Paul Revere was a prime mover and the first president. The association's aims were charitable, prudential, and social. The service most valued was performed by the Funeral Fund, for subscribers' widows or orphans, who would be waited upon by the treasurer with a payment of forty dollars and 'with such consolatory observations as the nature of the case may seem to require.' At the annual meeting in December a public festival was called for by the constitution and much of the association's annals are involved with these affairs — their distinguished guests, odes, toasts, songs, addresses, and unpaid bills.

In the same general mold and with comparable aims in view, the Boston journeyman printers finally organized themselves in 1824 as the Franklin Typographical Society, inspired by the example of New York, whence some of the founding members came.

---

[5] The ode at the 1807 dinner, written for the occasion and read by Robert Treat Paine, Jr., did good service for many years at such gatherings. That year's oration, delivered by John Russell, was titled 'The History and Importance of the Printing Art.'

[6] Joseph T. Buckingham, who joined the Association in 1811, compiled its history as *Annals of the Massachusetts Charitable Mechanic Association* (Boston, 1853). See the constitution on pp. 6 ff.

Their association served to relieve sick members and to provide 'for the decent interment of such as were removed by death.' Accordingly, as with the Mechanic Association, great care was taken to see that the membership rolls were not encumbered with the intemperate and unthrifty. 'No man known to be of dissipated habits, or suspected of disreputable conduct in any respect, could obtain admission.' In mid-January the society would invite the proprietors of printing-offices (whose contributions to the welfare funds were always welcome), foremen, editors, and civic dignitaries, to join them in the celebration of Franklin's birthday. The address, the songs and poems, the numerous and ingenious punning 'sentiments,' extolled Ars Artium, or 'the craft,' and its practitioners in the highest terms. And sometimes when the proceedings were published the printer was moved to exceptional efforts in the way of planning, composition, presswork, decorative treatment, and the selection of materials. An instance is the thirty-two page booklet containing Jefferson Clark's *Address Delivered at the Anniversary Celebration of the Franklin Typographical Society* printed by Dutton and Wentworth. The printers placed a cap on their good work by setting forth on the last page the elaborate 'Here lieth the outer form of Typography Page' from Johnson's *Typographia* (London, 1824).[7] Later a

---

[7] This *Address* (Boston, 1826) contains also a hymn, 'The Art of Printing' by Thomas G. Fessenden, and a song, 'The Press,' from the same prolific bard. In addition there are a note on the origin of the Society, the usual outpouring of toasts, and more notes with particular reference to Johnson's *Typographia*. Details of the history of the Society are sketched by Thomas Gill in the *Proceedings* (Boston, 1848) recording the address, poems, speeches, etc., of the Printers' Festival on January 15 of that year. The official records of the Franklin Typographical Society were destroyed by fire (Rollo G. Silver, *The Boston Book Trade 1800–1825*, New York, 1949, p. 11), along with those of the early journeyman's union organizations of Boston. See Ethelbert

course of lectures was offered to members and in 1830 a lending library was established which by mid-century contained five hundred volumes and whose catalogue of 1873 and five supplements list more than twenty-five hundred volumes.

Boston is credited with the fourth 'book club' in the country — the first being The Junto, formed by Benjamin Franklin in Philadelphia — and this club, like the Junto, owed its existence to the initiative of printers.[8] In 1803 Edmund Munroe and David Francis took over *The Monthly Anthology, or Magazine of Polite Literature* from its editor, discouraged after six months. Being young and enterprising they determined to carry on. They interested William Emerson in it and under his guidance the magazine was continued and, in October of 1805, the Anthology Society formed to support it. The fourteen charter members soon decided that they needed a library. Next year they established a reading room, to which more than a hundred of the 'liberal gentlemen of Boston' subscribed. The society meanwhile was publishing its *Monthly Anthology and Boston Review.*

'The Society, thus formed, maintained its existence with reputation for about six years, and issued ten octavo volumes from the press, constituting one of

Stewart, 'A Documentary History of the Early Organizations of Printers,' *Bulletin of the Bureau of Labor*, No. 61 (Washington, 1905).

The example of typographic punning in the mock *hic jacet* of Typography Page doubtless put the American word-players on their mettle. Their 'sentiments' or toasts at the 1826 meeting included the following terms: wet down, lye trough, gallows, mackle, twelve quire tokens, bar, ribs, worked off, old shoe, minion, monks and friars. A sample toast: 'The Franklin Typographical Society — An Association of Compositors and Pressmen — may the *bodies* be *equal* in *sorts*, and the *forms* well *locked up* in friendship.' The habit persisted at Society festivals through the middle of the century.

[8] Adolf Growoll, *American Book Clubs* (New York, 1897). Through Joel Barlow and his *Columbiad*, New England printers have a share in the second club, the Hartford Wits.

the most lasting and honorable monuments of the taste and literature of the period. Its labors may be considered as a true revival of polite learning in this country, after that decay and neglect, which resulted from the distractions of the Revolutionary War, and as forming an epoch in the intellectual history of the United States.' [9]

The Anthology Society's library and reading room soon outgrew the modest plan for them. In 1807 a charter was secured organizing them under the now illustrious title of The Boston Athenæum, an institution known today for its friendly relations with printers. Its own printing reflects this special interest.

But in the early decades of the nineteenth century there was no body of critical authority and taste, let alone princely patronage, to encourage workmen to venture beyond the unmarked boundary where craftsmanship becomes art. With the Anthology Society there had emerged the beginning of self-criticism, but directed toward literature rather than visual art, although the *Monthly* would occasionally speak of an edition as 'elegant' or 'handsome.' Books to feed Boston's great intellectual appetite were in demand always but, except for a sound portrait, a good family likeness by Copley or by Gilbert Stuart say, the love of pictures and other refinements appreciated by the bibliophile made slow headway against the puritan tradition. Obadiah Rich went to London to set up his rare book business, after having become immersed in collecting fine and rare Spanish works as consul at Valencia in 1815. Henry Stevens 'of Vermont' presently followed in his footsteps.

Whenever a printer or publisher — the careers now were less frequently combined in the same individual — did go out of his way to make a book or job at-

[9] Josiah Quincy, *History of the Boston Athenæum* (Cambridge, 1851), p. 3.

tractive, the favorite means was illustration. So had Boston's first printer, John Foster, getting out William Hubbard's *Narrative of the Troubles with the Indians in New-England* in 1677, cut the 'White Hills' map on a wood-block to begin book illustration in the British American colonies. So had Isaiah Thomas embellished his folio Bible of 1791 with fifty plates on copper by a four-man Yankee team. The strait-laced literary *Monthly Anthology*, rather poorly printed by Munroe and Francis, was dressed up in a copperplate title-page by Joseph Callender. The typographical glories of *The Columbiad* were accompanied by highly polished plates from abroad, but in Boston for Jacob Bigelow's *American Medical Botany*, 1817–1820, a new peak of ingenuity was attained. In the first part the engraver, William B. Annin, rendered in line the illustrations drawn and colored as the author said 'principally' by himself. The prints were then painted to match Dr. Bigelow's original. As the work progressed through the three volumes containing sixty plates, however, a technique new to America (and with it Annin's new partner, George G. Smith) put in an appearance.[10] With line, the engravers introduce aquatint to convey the modeling of stems, leaves, and so forth. Then the appropriate inks are dabbed on, e.g., green for foliage, red for petals, blue for berries, and the three-color print pulled in one impression. Additional bits of color as required are touched in with a brush. It could not be claimed that the process was carefree, but it doubtless enabled the plate printers to control the reproductions more closely and saved much painstaking hand painting of the prints.

[10] Silver, *The Boston Book Trade*, p. 13: 'This three-volume work . . . contained plates printed in color — one of the first, if not the first, so printed in America.'

The letterpress of *American Medical Botany*, by Hilliard and Metcalf of the University Press, Cambridge, supports our thesis that the ambitious leaps in bookmaking of the period were expressed in pictorial rather than typographic terms — *The Columbiad* and certain other achievements in Philadelphia and New York notwithstanding. The type-face foretokens the plague of thickened-up fonts which was spreading over the land with the rise in emphasis on jobbing work, though the present english size from Binny & Ronaldson is not yet a 'fat-face.' The composition fails chiefly by reason of overwide word spacing, and uneven inking and presswork further indicate that this reputable printing-office simply lacked the knowledge and skill to transform decent types and paper into a book typographically worthy of its quite exceptional illustrations.

The industrial revolution, signaled by the eruptions of organizing and newly articulate groups of printers, was becoming manifest on every hand in the application of inventions and more precise methods to the bookmaking 'arts' — art being then sensibly defined as doing or making as distinguished from science or knowing. The sharp rise of labor costs helped turn the pervading scientific attitude toward developing more efficient tools and methods. But in its teens the century was not ready to exploit what American inventive genius produced. Jacob Perkins of Newburyport, whose name is inscribed on the walls of the Massachusetts Institute of Technology with those of other illustrious persons, was constrained to export the invention of a hardening and softening process which made practicable engraving on and printing from steel plates.[11] Then there was William Church of

[11] As early as 1801 Perkins applied his invention to the making of Massachusetts banknotes and, with Gideon Fairman, he was publishing

Boston, a native Vermonter, who invented — and patented in England in 1822 — the first machine for casting type, in combination with his projects for mechanical composition and a one-man speeded-up hand press.[12] Meanwhile in Boston a series of experiments looked to the mechanization of printing: as early as 1811–1812 John B. Sawin and Thomas B. Wait were reported busy with 'circular' and 'cylindrical' presses and Daniel Treadwell was by 1822 building his one-horse-power presses — powered by one horse.[13] The steam power bed-and-platen press which Isaac Adams invented in 1830 and improved in 1836 became the favorite of American book and good jobbing printers for a generation. At the same time Stephen P. Ruggles developed his Ruggles Card Press, prototype of all small platen jobbers. During this period in other places papermaking machines, both of the Gilpin type from which the first continuous roll of American paper came in 1817 and of the Fourdrinier type introduced in the late twenties, began to take up the task of furnishing the increasingly voracious presses. The plating of typographic materials by the stereotype process, in New York as early as 1811, was followed by electrotyping at the opening of the forties.

Stereographic Copies printed from 'patent steel plates' within two years thereafter. After trying his fortune in Philadelphia, he went to London in 1818 to enter his process, combined with Asa Spencer's for lathework patterns, in the Bank of England's competition for a banknote secure from counterfeit. The attempt failed because a clever wood-engraver there was able to duplicate the Perkins specimen. Thomas Bewick's *Memoir* (London, 1862) contains his account of the affair.

[12] Thomas C. Hansard, *Typographia* (London, 1825) devotes pages 665–677 to Dr. Church's 'chimeras.'

[13] The most distinguished of American iron hand presses, the Columbian, was apparently not well known in Boston. The inventor, George Clymer, a Philadelphian, won the praises of New York and home town printers but he soon (1817) went abroad to manufacture this gaudily decorative and mechanically excellent press. The story is told by Jacob Kainen, *George Clymer and the Columbian Press* (New York, 1950).

Unfortunately there is no clear correlation between the artistic quality of print and the mechanical means of its production. The decline of peak standards in English printing set in, for example, closely following introduction of the vastly more efficient Stanhopian press and composition inking rollers. Was this the result of that 'softening' which is supposed to demoralize workmen whenever technological advances replace an awkward laborious process with a simpler, better one? Whatever the cause no one can deny the reality: there were the triumphs of William Bulmer, of Thomas Bensley, of the greatly exciting 'Macklin Bible.' Then came on the Duke of Roxburghe's sale and the bibliomaniacal frenzy, the opulent concern with fine printing by princely patrons and members of the club of 'highly respected and exalted characters' (as wistfully noticed by the Boston journeymen in the attempt to transcend their usual standard), and with it all, the decline.[14] The man is more consequential than the machine; as a modern American printer mused in the workroom of a sixteenth-century master, 'From these uncouth unions of wood and stone, pinned together with bits of iron, he made his pressmen extort workmanship which has been the admiration of the world.'

There was no Roxburghe Club, no Thomas Frognall Dibdin, no William Pickering–Charles Whittingham team in America to hold out against the general nineteenth-century relapse. But George Ticknor and presently William Hickling Prescott and others were developing talents as internationally respected collectors and scholarly bookmen. And still more sig-

---

[14] Franklin Typographical Society *Address* (Boston, 1826), p. 27. See note 7.

The quotation which follows is from Theodore L. De Vinne, 'The Plantin-Moretus Museum at Antwerp,' first published as 'A Printer's Paradise' in *The Century Magazine* for June 1888.

nificantly, though unrecognized, in the hinterland
newspaper offices were developing the few printers
who, besides educating themselves, learned thoroughly all departments of the trade and then, as
master printers, practiced it as a profession and an
art. The Northfield, Massachusetts, boy Joel Munsell
(1808–1880), who printed with distinction in Albany
and also studied, collected books, and wrote valuable
works of authority in his chosen field, is one example.
Another is the more celebrated Theodore Low De
Vinne (1828–1914), whose career spanned the trans-
formation of printing from a small hand operation to
the mechanized and industrialized conditions of the
twentieth century. A driving businessman and an
exacting craftsman, he became one of the keenest
scholars of all time in printing. In these men the
printer rose to his traditional status as man of letters,
superior to the divisive tendencies of industrial de-
partmentalization.

More and more attention, however, was devoted
to printing for commerce, — 'the nearer the bone,
the sweeter the meat' — further confounding the
confusion between book and jobbing practice. The
latter field was the one of opportunity, inviting supple
and venturesome printers because in this line of work
a clever man with light equipment and small fonts
of 'fat-faces' and novelties might thrive along with
the well-established house. Among industries to be
served was that of the typefounder. Boston had two
firms, of which the earliest to set up shop was the
Boston Type & Stereotype Foundry, begun as a
branch of the New York foundry of Elihu White in
1817. The New England Type Foundry was established in 1824. Both issued nicely printed specimen
books of their types during the twenties. At the first
exhibition of the Massachusetts Charitable Mechanic

Association in 1837 the Boston Type Foundry was awarded a silver medal for the 'beauty of face and durability of metal' possessed by its products.[15] Dutton and Wentworth received a silver medal, too, the citation singling out their printing of the Boston Type Foundry's specimen book as 'the best specimen of job work exhibited.' Henry Willis of the rival house submitted three type specimen books on this occasion, 'affording a great variety, of the various sizes, of good taste and handsome cut' as the judges found, though they made no award. The several hopeful printers of the Waverley Novels in twenty-seven volumes, of a seven-volume Shakespeare and two-volume Milton, of the lives of Franklin and of Washington, received some compliments and nothing more.

The era of revival in the arts following the War of 1812 and preceding the Civil War included no golden day of printing comparable to that of literature around Boston. In the earlier phases the printers set title pages like their display advertisements in lines alternating bold and light, solid and open, with brusquely contrasting thicks and thins in rules and face of types. Arresting and occasionally handsome combinations were achieved, but more often on the publicity wrapper of a book than inside. The type-founders offered a profusion of ornamental stock cuts and 'Greek revival' borders. The copperplate engravers' contrasts were at last exceeded with a vengeance, but presently the positive and frequently brash or awkward fashion took a turn in the direction of misty refinement. It matched the self-consciousness of the young literati of the forties and keyed in with the grey or colored lithographs softly illuminating

[15] *First Exhibition and Fair of the Massachusetts Charitable Mechanic Association, at Faneuil and Quincy Halls, in the City of Boston, September 18, 1837* (Boston, 1837), p. 56.

the gift books and sentimental annuals, which absorbed the cleverest skills and best machines of the industry. By mid-century even the traditionally hardheaded typefounders had learned to speak of their novelty fonts as 'poetic.'

Boston's book-collecting and scholarly habits formed the best anchor to windward. The young men of wealth and education who grew up in the first quarter of the nineteenth century to be the first scholarly authorities cultivated a fine New England tradition.[16] A bookman like George Ticknor made wholesome demands upon his printers; also he could appreciate their efforts, as when in the preface to his *History of Spanish Literature*, 1849, he cites the University Press of Cambridge and 'Mr. George Nichols, its scholarlike corrector, for the practised skill and conscientious fidelity' of their part in the work, rather than the New York publishers. It is a soundly made three-decker, in Dickinson's excellent Scotch face firmly and evenly impressed on good paper, though the imposition makes improper margins.[17] The 1855 work, *History of the Reign of Philip*

[16] Already in the seventeenth century Increase Mather had collected more than a thousand volumes. Elias Hasket Derby bought 'an elegant library' of six hundred volumes in 1783 from his London bookseller and later purchased seven hundred French books. John Pickering had four thousand volumes. William Bentley possessed five thousand. Joseph S. Buckminster was another important early collector whose books, sold in 1812, realized prices higher than any estimate (riding the wave of the Roxburghe sale in London).

[17] Samuel Nelson Dickinson, typefounder, printer and publisher, was born in 1801 at Phelps, Ontario County, New York, and served his apprenticeship on the Geneva *Palladium*. He came to Boston about 1828 and worked as compositor for the Boston Type and Stereotype Foundry and, the year after, set up as a master printer. According to De Vinne, *The Practice of Typography: A Treatise on . . . Plain Printing Types* (New York, 1900), p. 104: 'Unable to get from any typefoundry of his city the types his taste demanded, he undertook to have them made. The style known as the Scotch-face was modelled by him in 1837, but cut and cast to his order by Alexander Wilson & Son, of Edinburgh. The matrices imported by him were the first types of the

the Second, by Ticknor's younger friend W. H. Prescott, published by Phillips, Samson and Company of Boston with the imprint of the 'printers to the University,' Metcalf and Company of Cambridge, as electrotypers, is not so distinguished.[18] 'Mr. Prescott loved his books almost as he loved his children'; his secretary, Edmund B. Otis, told Ticknor 'he liked to see them well dressed, in rich, substantial bindings, and if one, by any accident, was dropped, "it annoyed him," he said jestingly, "almost as much as if a baby fell."' The historian's interest in details is indicated by such entries in his journal as this: 'Have received an English copy of "Ferdinand and Isabella." Better paper, blacker ink, more showy pages, but, on the whole, not so good type. . . .'[19]

When, on the death of Prescott in 1859, it fell to George Ticknor's lot to prepare a memoir, the result was a proper bookman's book. The *Life of William Hickling Prescott* is a quarto very carefully made at

Dickinson Foundry in 1839, and were received with marked favor. The first specimen-book of the Dickinson Foundry, published in 1842, shows a refined taste and marked ability, and served as a stimulus to other founders. . . .' Also, according to De Vinne, p. 212: 'The plan or design for the peculiar style known as the Scotch-face was first originated in 1837 by S. N. Dickinson of Boston. Alexander Wilson & Son cut the punches to his order and so made the first "Scotch-face" types. Matrices from these punches were imported by the designer, who cast from them in 1839 the first types made in his new foundry.' In Dickinson's specimen book of 1847 are three kinds of Scotch face which, as the preface states, were American cut and 'considered by many as very handsome.' His *Typographic Advertiser,* beginning with the issue of November 1845, preceded that of the Johnson foundry with the same title by ten years. The *Printers' Monthly Bulletin* of the Boston Type Foundry began in January of 1858.

[18] Prescott also could be generous in appreciation of a printer's efforts. His private memorandum, on publication of the *History of the Reign of Ferdinand and Isabella* (London, 1838), stated that among the chief factors in its success were 'the beautiful dress and mechanical execution of the book.' As a matter of fact, the work is not above reproach in these respects.

[19] George Ticknor, *Life of William Hickling Prescott* (Boston, 1864), pp. 466, 118 (the latter entry was dated July 27, 1838).

the University Press of Welch, Bigelow, and Company of Cambridge. There is of course an engraved portrait frontispiece and opposite is an airy title page set in A. C. Phemister's new modernized old-style. Inside the book are a number of remarkable features in an American production of Civil War times. The body of the work is set throughout in a Caslonish old-style with long ſ and ct ligatures. (The revival had already been signaled by the appearance of a similar letter that turned up from somewhere in the Boston Type Foundry *Printers' Monthly Bulletin* for January 1858 to illustrate the Bay Psalm Book style.) [20] Besides the intaglio engravings there are many fine wood-engraved vignettes illustrating the text and embellishing the chapter openings, and it is proudly announced that the initial letters and headpiece blocks were especially engraved from original designs. Perhaps the most unusual feature of all is the imposition; the Prescott memoir has decent margins.

The same press was capable of turning out books not so impeccably grand but rather more charming. A nice example is Whittier's *Snow-Bound* published by Ticknor (George's cousin) and Fields, 1868. A prefatory note inside a lozenge of rules advertises that the book was prepared under supervision of the

---

[20] L. Johnson & Company's *Typographic Advertiser* for January 1859, p. 104, printed some eighteenth-century verse after this introduction: 'This Brevier is a specimen of our old-style type, from originals got up more than a century ago. Small Pica is also ready for order; and other sizes are in preparation.' In the July issue the small pica is used for Thomas MacKellar's verses headed 'Ye Poet illustrateth Men's Callynges' in quaint chapbook costume; it reappears in the advertisement on p. 120. The October number devotes two pages to a showing of thirteen sizes from nonpareil to two-line pica of this face, now called Old Style.

In England the Pickering-Whittingham alliance had been introducing Caslon's Old Face into appropriate display lines since 1840 and by 1844 were setting an entire book (George Herbert, *The Temple*) in that face. The same types were imported by Joel Munsell of Albany who, in 1856, used them for printing *Papers Relating to the Island of Nantucket*.

Boston wood-engraver A. V. S. Anthony. An associate in the work was William J. Linton, author of *The History of Wood-Engraving in America*.[21]

Meanwhile Henry O. Houghton, who, following his printing apprenticeship on the Burlington, Vermont, *Free Press*, had been working as a proofreader in the Dickinson foundry, now established his beachhead on the opposite bank of the Charles. To the business he brought some of the old-time printer's sense of literary vocation. This, with sound capabilities augmented by a knack for strategy that was particularly valuable in picking partners, soon led to his highly successful invasion of the publishing field. The Riverside Press at the same time earned a just fame for printing and continued to give abundant evidence of the boss's interest in that department. Houghton was a constant student of the early masterpieces of European printing and thereby developed an exceptionally sure taste and a discerning eye for form.[22]

[21] Linton, in *The History of Wood-Engraving in America* (London, 1882), p. [34], points out the exceptional printing abilities of A. K. P. Welch of the University Press, especially in connection with a state-sponsored publication, Harris' *Insects Injurious to Vegetation*, with exquisite illustrations engraved on wood by Henry Marsh. In the seventies S. S. Kilburn, designer and engraver on wood, advertised that he was 'prepared to undertake the pictorial department of any book, however illustrated, or to furnish the whole illustrations of a pictorial newspaper, both in designs and engravings, with the promptness the Press demands.' His *Specimen of Designing and Engraving on Wood* displays new glories wrested from woodblocks, with the help of A. Holland, 'wood cut and color printer,' and fine smooth paper.

[22] The outstanding case in point is that of the Bell types called English Copper-face by The Riverside Press specimen of 1887 (later christened Brimmer by Bruce Rogers and Mountjoye by D. B. Updike). The story is told in Stanley Morison's *John Bell, 1745–1831* (Cambridge, Eng., 1930), pp. 127–136 (Appendix c): Houghton was visiting England in 1864, spotted the fine Bell types, and brought the face home to lead the revival of its use after long neglect. This does not, however, explain earlier appearance of the same design in the Boston neighborhood; e.g., the english roman was used for display throughout the Ticknor and Fields catalogue printed at The Riverside Press and dated November 1858.

When Richard Grant White's edition of Shakespeare appeared, the *Printers' Monthly Bulletin*, January 1860, in behalf of the Boston Type Foundry which furnished the types, did not neglect the 'Riverside Printing Establishment' in distributing praise to all concerned: 'The *Athenaeum*, which rarely finds anything American which it does not abuse' had said: 'We have in England, among books regularly published, nothing to compare with it for goodness of paper and beauty of type. It is a credit to the American trade.' This tribute from abroad had already been circulated by the Boston *Transcript*. But there is plenty of Houghton's book production, such as James Francis Child's *English & Scottish Popular Ballads*, 1882, or *A Book of the Tile Club*, 1886, that can speak for itself without asking foreign favors. He was instrumental in laying down foundations for the best American bookmaking achievement of the late nineteenth and early twentieth centuries.

Another important figure was John Wilson. With his grown son, also John, he had come from Glasgow, by way of Belfast, and begun working for Dickinson in 1846, the same year that Houghton made his beginning there. The elder Wilson was a scholarly printer and author of a standard work on punctuation. It was natural for him to gravitate to the neighborhood of Harvard University, where he and his son established themselves as printers right after the Civil War. Harvard conferred an honorary M.A. on the senior Wilson in 1866. He died in 1868. Ten years later the son, with Charles E. Wentworth as partner, bought the University Press. They continued using John Wilson & Son as firm name in combination with the new title.[23]

[23] The University Press had no official tie with Harvard, although at this period it enjoyed the goodwill of the university's president and

Shortly before the merger a young German immigrant named Carl H. Heintzemann came to work for John Wilson. He brought to the trade an exceptional background — his father had been a schoolmaster in Germany for half a century and the two sons were brought up with a devotion to books and the arts — together with the requisite capabilities and strength of purpose to make it effective. He mastered the business with Teutonic thoroughness but his heart was lost to the arts and he practiced printing in their light and spirit, *con amore,* as he loved performing (very competently) on his piano. In 1879, at twenty-five, he set up shop for himself on the corner of School Street where the Five Cents Savings Bank now is. The young editor of the English High School *Record,* Henry Lewis Johnson, found him there in 1886. For Johnson already had set forth on what the *Record* spoke of as 'the inky road to the stars' and was looking for better printing. His enthusiasm and keenness to learn brought him into close relations with the Heintzemann house for many years to come.[24]

faculty for whom much of its work was done. Harvard University entered the printing field apparently only in 1871 when a small office was set up to print examination papers and other forms. See Hellmut Lehmann-Haupt, *The Book in America,* 2nd ed. (New York, 1951), p. 185. According to Buckingham's notes on the Faustus Association (see note 4 above): 'William Hilliard, when he joined the association, was "printer to the university" at Cambridge. He was a native of that town, son of the Rev. Timothy Hilliard, minister of the First Congregational Church. The types, presses, and other furniture of the office with which he began business, were owned by the corporation of the college. . . . He was an excellent printer.' In 1805 Hilliard took into partnership Eliab W. Metcalf, who 'acquired a handsome property, which he left to his family in 1837.'

[24] Carl H. Heintzemann was born at Wildungen in Prussia on December 28, 1854. His life and work were the subject of a projected monograph which intermittently occupied the attention of the Society of Printers for twenty years but was never carried through. Following a suggestion by C. P. Rollins at the February 1924 meeting such a pub-

The cultural climate of the Boston which Carl Heintzemann became part of had changed markedly from that of pre-Civil War times. In 1870 the Museum of Fine Arts was established as an institutional expression of the zest for art then taking possession of all levels of society. As Van Wyck Brooks draws the picture in *New England: Indian Summer 1865–1915* (p. 153): a 'vogue of travel went hand in hand with the ever-growing rage for art that characterized the younger generation. Young men of means roamed over Italy, inspired with a wish to see sincerely, the fruit of their reading of Ruskin. They copied Roman inscriptions in their pocket notebooks.' Thanks largely to the efforts of George Ticknor, the Boston Public Library had already come into being and was making constant gains — that could be discounted in bookish Boston — but when the Boston Symphony was founded in 1881 another aesthetic frontier was taken. As standard bearer of the movement, Charles Eliot Norton (1827–1908), an intimate friend of John Ruskin, occupied somewhat the same position in this

---

lication was authorized and a committee appointed with G. P. Winship as chairman. There was much talk and many unavailing attempts to revive the project until the chairman finally discharged his conscience of it at the annual meeting of May 1944. This story is told in more detail in Chapter III.

In connection with this effort, Johnson was actively gathering materials in 1933, as shown by a letter to him of June 8 that year from a daughter, Helen Heintzemann Bevan. Recalling her father's devotion to his piano, she wrote: 'He would sometimes play for hours at a time working over a certain passage which he wouldn't give up even for his meals. Many times he would bring his sheet of music to the dinner table and lay it down beside his plate and study it between bites.' His sons Charles and George both became members of the Society. Others in the organization who as apprentices or otherwise came much under his influence include Johnson, Dwiggins, Rollins, James G. Clarke, and A. F. Mackay through whose efforts a memorial page was contributed to the 1924 Craftsmen Number of *The American Printer*. The same journal, in the issue for May 1901, contained 'The Work of the Heintzemann Press' by George French. Heintzemann died in Boston on August 11, 1908.

country that the English critic and reformer did in his. They shared the same interest in printing as a craft having more possibilities for the cause of spiritual regeneration than those buried deeper in industrialism.

Among those sensing the opportunities of this movement was a man of artistic inclinations and organizing ability named Arthur B. Turnure. He had set up with the Gilliss Press in New York, at the end of the seventies, what amounted to a fine printing and bookmaking department. He called it the Art Age Press. One of its first and grandest productions was a *Catalogue of the Art Department of the New England Manufacturers' and Mechanics' Institute* (Boston, 1883). The Institute, incorporated in 1879, was promoted as a rival of the venerable Massachusetts Charitable Mechanic Association. An advertisement of the Art Age Press makes this apology:

Mr. Arthur B. Turnure has to state that this catalogue of the New England Manufacturers' and Mechanics' Institute was made in six weeks. Had the work been undertaken by him before the summer season more special artists might have been engaged for designing head bands, initials, and tail pieces, and otherwise embellishing the book. As it is, Mr. Turnure has drawn freely from the best foreign sources—art journals and special publications—in ornamenting the pages.

The modest cough notwithstanding, this catalogue measuring a foot tall and three-quarters of an inch thick made a stir. Carefully printed in modernized old-style types on smooth 'art' paper, with rubricated title and a highly ornamented and colored wrapper, the book is in three main divisions: a catalogue of exhibits numbering seven hundred thirty-one items, illustrations from original drawings and prints, and

articles by twenty-one authorities on various aspects
of American art. The success of this venture enabled
Turnure to spend the following summer abroad on
the proceeds.[25]

Art Year Book 1884, 'prepared and published by
the New England Institute,' is successor to the *Catalogue* and likewise a product of Turnure's Art Age
Press. According to the preface, 'The object of this
publication is to present to the world a volume, in
which the highest American art products of the year
are represented by means of suitable graphic arts, and
produced entirely by means of American brains, labor
and materials ...' The catalogue listing this time
was relegated to the back of the case-bound volume.
The illustrations are eleven examples of various
graphic processes including wood-engraving, lithography, albertype, phototype, and artotype repre-

[25] Walter Gilliss in *Recollections of the Gilliss Press* (New York, 1926)
tells how the Gilliss brothers became acquainted with Turnure at the
time they began printing *Art Interchange* in 1878, 'an acquaintance
which was destined to develop into a close friendship, and, later on,
into a partnership.' Turnure was a bibliophile and soon he began seeing
special books and pamphlets through the Gilliss plant under an Art
Interchange imprint. After selling his interest in that periodical he
started a new monthly, *The Art Age*, 'devoted to the practical development of the art idea as applied in certain trades, manufactures and our
every-day necessities; and of value particularly to those who are interested in typographic art, current art, literature and occasional publications of note.' He continued even more actively producing work, at
the Gilliss Press, with the Art Age imprint. His need for a showroom
in which to exhibit superior printing — not least that of the Art Age
Press — led him to make the first move in the organization of the
Grolier Club. See John T. Winterich, *The Grolier Club 1884–1950, An
Informal History* (New York, 1950).

Van Wyck Brooks, *New England: Indian Summer* (New York, 1940),
p. 345 n.: 'There was a marked revival of interest in the arts and crafts,
in textiles, pottery, etc., in the years round 1880. This reaction against
machine-methods was further stimulated by the visit of Oscar Wilde in
1882. Longfellow's *Keramos*, 1877, appeared when the interest in
ceramics was reviving....' This was the year that the Tile Club of
New York artists was formed; nine years later their sumptuous *Book*
came from The Riverside Press.

sented by four reproductions of wash drawings printed in colored inks. A decorative page drawn by Howard Pyle announces 'notes descriptive and biographic' which take the place of the articles published the year before. The extravagant *chinoiserie* of the title page, and the cover of decorated paper on beveled boards, are the work of George R. Halm, who, after serving an apprenticeship as wood-engraver with Anthony, had located in a New York studio as a professional designer of book decoration. 'To this branch he was one of the first to give attention . . .' Notice is further taken of bookmaking advances during the year, gauged by willingness of publishers to venture into the field of well-made limited editions, and of the founding that spring of the Grolier Club 'having for its object the literary study and promotion of the arts entering into the production of books.' It is pointed out that the rough-edged paper used for the beginning of the book 'is a hand-made fabric from the L. L. Brown Paper Co., who are said to be the only makers in this country of hand-made papers. Their mill has been manufacturing this paper for about a year, stimulus being given by the introduction of limited editions, the supply for which has come heretofore from Holland, France and England.'

Other manifestations of the awakening aesthetic consciousness appeared in the form of clubs. A group of young men interested in the arts and learned professions, much under the influence of Professor Norton, organized themselves as the Tavern Club of Boston. In 1887 bibliophiles joined forces to found the Club of Odd Volumes for 'the promotion of Literary and Artistic Tastes, the Study of the Arts as applied to Book-making, the establishment and maintenance of a Reference Library, and Exhibits of a special or instructive character.' This statement of aims was presently amplified to include the publishing program which has contributed a number of important — and nicely produced — books about books. Throughout its distinguished history the club has quietly served to uphold good standards of bookmaking by means of discussions and exhibitions devoted to the subject and — at a still more vital point — by commissioning work from able designers and presses to meet critical standards of excellence.

Meanwhile Henry Lewis Johnson, who had stayed on for another year as editor of the *Record* after graduation from English High School in June 1885, became the editor and publisher of the Hyde Park *Times*. In 1887 he was publisher of *The Agents' Journal*, 'published monthly in the interests of agents, inventors and dealers.' Then he studied two years at M.I.T. as a member of the class of 1892, and characteristically turns up as publisher of *Photogravure Views of the Mass. Institute of Technology*, 1889, produced by the Boston Photogravure Company. With this firm's backing, early in 1891 he began bringing out *The Engraver and Printer*, 'a monthly magazine of progress in illustration.' The 'art idea' in printing took a long step in the pages of this journal.

In England, William Morris was at the head of the movement. Under the dynamic leadership of the Kelmscott master, the 'Morris revival' soon was reverberating on these shores. *The Knight Errant*, gotten out by Ralph Adams Cram and Bertram Grosvenor Goodhue, Herbert Copeland, Fred Holland Day, and Francis Watts Lee, was an immediate and splendid response from Boston.[26] The large quarto on

[26] *A Quarter-Yearly Review of the Liberal Arts Called The Knight Errant. Being a Magazine of Appreciation.* Printed for the Proprietors at the Elzevir Press, Boston, A.D. MDCCCXCII. In an opening 'apology' in the April 1892 number, the editors ask what other course is open than 'to return ... to that time when beauty began to fade

handmade paper, with a title page by Goodhue suggested by Dürer's 'Knight, Death and Devil,' made its appearance in the spring of 1892 (less than a year after publication in England of the first Kelmscott Press book), mixing typographical considerations with Bernard Berenson's comment on Correggio and with Richard Hovey's poems. In the final number, October 1894, among the book and bookmaking notices, attention is directed toward the work of Daniel Berkeley Updike; 'an Altar-book, now in preparation by him ... will be perhaps the finest book ever published in this country. . . .'

As F. H. Day in the preceding number of *The Knight Errant* (p. 95) remarked, 'Messrs. Houghton & Mifflin have done more for us in their conservative way toward the improvement of the art of bookmaking than any other six houses' and in 1880 the young Updike at twenty had begun with them the twelve-year term which preceded his setting up inde-

from life, not to restore a fictitious and evanescent similitude of things that were, but to learn the underlying principles of that great time, wherewith the times to come must have far closer kinship than with the things that be.' An article by Charles Eliot Norton expresses his gentle aesthetic pessimism. More directly pertinent is Francis Watts Lee's article in the July number, 'Some Thoughts upon Beauty in Typography Suggested by the Work of Mr. William Morris at the Kelmscott Press,' concluding with his approving quotation that the Morris books were 'the crowning glory of the nineteenth century.' Much of the review is devoted to bookish and printing concerns. An epilogue to the final issue explains that the subscription list had never paid the expenses and therefore 'we are in the bog, horse and man.' The last of the four numbers came out in October 1894, more than two years after the initial issue in April 1892. 'The *Knight Errant* might have been justly termed quixotic had it ventured, a year ago, to prophesy a movement in the direction of really good bookmaking in America' observes this final issue, allowing the mood of pessimism to be lifted by the appearance of Copeland and Day, and of Stone and Kimball, who 'have recently begun business with the avowed intention of publishing only fine books.' Rossetti's *House of Life* with borders 'much better drawn than many of those from the Kelmscott press' and Santayana's *Lucifer* are praised as auspicious beginnings respectively by these two firms.

pendently as a designer and typographical consultant. 'The time spent at the Riverside Press had convinced me that I must do something on my own lines,' he recalled forty years later, 'and through a commission to print an *Altar Book*, which my old friend the late Harold Brown of Rhode Island stood ready to finance, the opportunity was offered.' He publicly offered his professional services in 1893 by means of two Kelmscott-style rubricated circulars. One of them was addressed simply 'To the Trade,' the other 'To the Clergy and Laity of the Episcopal Church and to All Others who are Interested in Ecclesiastical Printing; Greeting.' [27] The following year Updike issued another circular 'printed in a type and manner highly complimentary to himself and to Mr. William Morris.' As *The Inland Printer* said in reproducing the first page, 'It is a treat to look upon'. *A Few Words about Printing, Book-making, and Their Allied Arts* was

[27] 'To the Trade. Mr. D. B. Updike, for the past twelve years with Houghton, Mifflin, & Co. of Boston and of The Riverside Press, Cambridge, has now severed his connection with that firm, and has opened an office of his own at number six Beacon Street, Boston.

'When with Houghton, Mifflin, and Company, Mr. Updike had charge of the preparation and arrangement of the catalogues, holiday bulletins, general circulars, advertising pages, posters, and other decorative printing, as well as of some of the books issued by that house. He is now prepared to undertake for such of the trade as desire it the same class of decorative printing and book-making. Typography and design in its relation thereto have long been Mr. Updike's special study, and he has also a practical knowledge of the commercial necessities of the work in which he is engaged. The following detailed statement of the various kinds of work that he undertakes may be of interest to Publishers, Booksellers, and Printers.' On the second and third pages under the headings 'Holiday Books,' 'Privately Printed Books,' 'Ecclesiastical Printing,' 'Decorations for Books,' '"Practical" Book-Covers,' and 'Minor Decorative Printing' he enumerated his specialties, e.g., 'limited editions of attractive little books of poems or essays printed on hand-made paper, with initials and bordered title-pages, in the modern aesthetic English manner'; clear, practical arrangement of genealogies; 'ecclesiastical printing of a rich yet simple sort'; title-pages and decorations in historical styles; preparation of attractive advertising matter.

Updike's report of a successful first year and an index to the progress of the new profession of book designer. His statement, dated October 15, 1894, began:

Among the arts and crafts in which persons of taste and cultivation have been increasingly interested during the past few years is that of printing, and design as applied thereto. The modern tendency to specialize the different portions of all work has been nowhere more apparent than in the printer's art, so that to-day the compositor no longer sets the styles of typography, but simply works under the direction of those who have made style in printing a special study. In other words, there are arising on every side, workers whose place is not that of the man by whom a printer's work is used, nor of the printer himself, but of one, who, by a knowledge of the requirements of clients on the one hand, and the abilities of the printer on the other, is able to produce a better result than either could alone. . . . Mr. Updike has for a long time past been chiefly interested in work of this kind, and he has been fitted by a very long practical experience to undertake it. . . .

His work, in so far as it concerns private persons, consists in carrying books through the press. . . . Mr. Updike's point of view is that of the amateur, but he endeavors to make his execution that of the professional, and so to direct the printer that the book will show the newest and best features of decorative work, with such special touches as make each book individual and suited to its purpose.

It is printed in black and red from the Dickinson Type Foundry's face later called Nicholas Jenson. Updike had been carrying on experiments with the manager of the foundry, Joseph Warren Phinney, toward reproducing Morris' Golden type for use in the Altar Book. The type was to have been Updike's exclusive property but, on a visit to Wilson's University Press, he saw proofs of it and learned that some of the type had been supplied them — even before he had finally approved the face and in spite of the understanding for its proprietary use. He had this one circular set up in it and printed by Wilson and never made use of it again. The opening initial letter A is in an ornamental panel running the full depth of the type page in the characteristic Goodhue manner. But meanwhile, in the January 1894 number of *The Engraver and Printer*, Updike had written 'The Black Art: A Homily,' raising an admonitory finger against 'the riotous use and abuse of new types in large sizes with sprawling ornaments, outline vignettes, and heraldic devices surrounded with borders of all degrees of splotchy blackness.' [28]

Early in the busy year of 1895, Joseph M. Bowles moved with his journal *Modern Art* from Indianapolis to Boston and a new publisher, L. Prang & Co. Soon after came Bruce Rogers, the young designer who had been contributing decorations to the magazine and arranging typography and illuminating texts for Bowles's publications. Next year Rogers was installed at The Riverside Press, through George H. Mifflin's interest in well-made books, and from 1900 till 1912 he had his own special department where he was responsible for planning and seeing through the press editions unequaled by the productions of any other American publisher.

Will H. Bradley, a native Bostonian who had

[28] Updike's 'homily,' slightly abridged, was issued as a separate pamphlet by The Camelot Press, Chicago, with a prologue by Fred. W. Goudy dated February 1895. Goudy and his partner, C. Lauron Hooper, were printers of *The Chap-Book*, published at Cambridge by Stone & Kimball. In the first number, May 15, 1894, Updike devoted a full page advertisement to the Altar Book. Of this period Goudy wrote: 'The *Chap-Book* opened my eyes to a new world; it brought me into contact through its pages with the writers and artists then high in the literary firmament.' In the 'prologue' to *The Black Art* he proclaimed: 'We have the enthusiasm of youth, the love of the quaint, and the desire for better things in printing.' See his *A Half Century of Type Design and Typography 1895-1945* (New York, 1946), p. 31 f.

drifted as a young printer to Chicago, came back at this time bringing a reputation as a designer of books and posters. His earliest book design, for *When Hearts Are Trumps*, commissioned by Stone & Kimball, had been executed at the University Press and published in March 1894. That year his work was broadcast among printers by *The Inland Printer* and in the Christmas issue appeared a panel of lettering which the American Type Founders Company picked up and presently named Bradley. Now he located at Springfield and, beginning with May 1896, issued the seven numbers of *Bradley His Book* from his Wayside Press.

Through October and November of 1895 an international poster show — ministering to a current rage — was held at the century-old Massachusetts Charitable Mechanic Association. Henry Lewis Johnson, writing in the December number of *The Engraver and Printer*, called this event 'the most important recognition which has been given to the art and influence of the poster.' It led up to his next major activity as organizer of the arts and crafts movement. The First Exhibition of Arts and Crafts was launched at the end of 1896 by the circulation of a proposal. On January 4, 1897, a meeting held at the Museum of Fine Arts established an advisory board and named Johnson as director. The date for the exhibition was set for April 5–17 in Copley Hall and a promotional piece decorated by Goodhue was circulated.[29] The response was enthusiastic. In the printing classification most of the entries were submitted by J. M.

[29] *First Exhibition of the Arts and Crafts, Copley Hall, Boston, April 5–17, MDCCCXCVII. Representing the Application of Art to Industry, and Comprising Manufactured Articles and Original Designs for the Same.* The board: General Charles G. Loring, Charles A. Cummings, Denman W. Ross, A. W. Longfellow, Jr., Ross Turner, C. Howard Walker, R. Clipston Sturgis, William Sturgis Bigelow, Sylvester Baxter, Henry Lewis Johnson, director.

Bowles, including examples of Bruce Rogers' work, and by D. B. Updike, of the Merrymount Press. The Heintzemann Press and the Wayside Press of Will Bradley were also represented. The catalogue had a cover design by Goodhue. It was at this exhibition that Mrs. Sarah W. Whitman (herself the designer of her friend Martin Brimmer's admired books), on confronting sample pages of the Tacitus printed in the rugged new Merrymount typeface, is reported by Updike to have ejaculated 'Phoebus, what a page!'

In the afterglow of this successful exhibition a committee was formed to act on the proposal of organizing a permanent association. With H. Langford Warren as chairman and Henry Lewis Johnson as secretary, the organization meeting was called for May 13, 1897. In quick succession the necessary steps were taken under Johnson's guidance to reach an agreement on the incorporation of The Society of Arts and Crafts and to equip it properly with by-laws and officers. Charles Eliot Norton was elected president, at the first meeting on October 13 following, by the twenty-four charter members.[30] In 1899 from the fourth to the fifteenth of April the society presented its first exhibition. The catalogue, with cover design by Theodore Brown Hapgood, Jr., indicates that the vigorous young organization was hitting its stride and that it held the continuing interest of its printing friends. After a quotation from William Morris the introduction states:

[30] The Society of Arts and Crafts incorporators were: Charles Eliot Norton, Arthur Astor Carey, C. Howard Walker, A. W. Longfellow Jr., Morris Gray, Henry Lewis Johnson, H. Langford Warren, Denman W. Ross, Robert D. Andrews, Ralph Adams Cram, Bertram Grosvenor Goodhue, Barton P. Jenks, D. B. Updike, Hugh Cairns, Mrs. D. D. Addison, Mrs. J. Montgomery Sears, Mrs. Henry Whitman, John Evans, I. Kirchmayer, George P. Kendrick, George R. Shaw, J. T. Coolidge Jr., Samuel D. Warren, George Edward Barton.

The Society of Arts and Crafts, in making this Exhibition, hopes that it may stimulate public interest in the lesser arts, and that it may aid in raising the standard of taste in the workman who makes and the public who buys. . . .

The century now drawing to a close has been marvellous for its mechanical and scientific development; but the very rapidity of this development and the conditions that made it possible have been adverse to the development of the fine arts. Indeed, with regard to the lesser arts of handicraft, we had almost reached the condition of forgetting that they might be fine arts at all, — they had, in fact, for the most part ceased to be such. . . .

II

Organization of the Printing Art Movement

WITH the turn of the century the strange *fin de siècle* compound of dainty halftone, ruggedly medieval, and more or less decadent 'art for art's sake' elements settled down to something more balanced, something nearer 'normal.' The admired nineteenth-century daintiness began to appear weak while, at the same time, a closer look at the Kelmscott models revealed that Jenson's roman, for example, was really a 'white' letter. As for smart-aleck aestheticism, it was due for decline and the remaining *art nouveau* oddities were dealt a sobering shock treatment by the Oscar Wilde scandal.

Normal is only another way of saying classical. Thomas Maitland Cleland's Cornhill Press period is of this time. In the upsurging humanism the leaders in interpreting printing style — Updike at the Merrymount Press and Rogers at The Riverside Press Department of Special Book-making — went on from Jenson to study Aldus, then Tory, and so forth. In working out their ideas they found Caslon's types very practical and, with an added dash of blackletter, quite gratifying.

Heintzemann, another Arts and Crafts enthusiast, surrounded himself at all times with artists and designers. His press was unofficial headquarters for those who looked at printing in an artistic light. He offered a *pied à terre* for wanderers like Bowles,

Bradley, and Johnson; a place for masters to work out their schemes and for apprentices to learn mastery. Bradley (who for the time being was setting up his Wayside Press as a department of the University Press) naturally sent to Heintzemann the young man too much in a hurry to finish his Harvard course. For Carl Purington Rollins at twenty-one with characteristic vigor and determination decided to be a printer. At case and stone and press he continued his education. He set up such things as *The Cornhill Booklet*. After hours he pursued recreational reading in Kelmscott editions at the Boston Public Library. He could stretch out the three-quarter hour nooning to contain a visit to Alfred Bartlett's shop on Cornhill and a glimpse of habitués like Chester Lane or Percy Grassby. Or he could cut across to Goodspeed's or Smith & McCance to browse away the precious minutes, or squander them with his good friend Frederic Allen Whiting, secretary of the Society of Arts and Crafts on Park Street. Nearly all his associates were 'masters' or 'craftsmen' of the society.[31]

Johnson was still on the council of the Society of Arts and Crafts and active in its interests but his heart was really in printing, the 'art idea' in printing.[32] Anyway he was a true pioneer — once the land

[31] An historical account is contained in *The Society of Arts & Crafts 1897–1924* by Mary R. Spain, a thirty-six page pamphlet published in 1924. Another publication of the Society, *Handicrafts*, supposed to be issued monthly, is a useful source of information. The earlier volumes were printed by the Heintzemann Press and then, after 1908, by Carl P. Rollins at his Dyke Mill, Montague, Massachusetts. There are early exhibition catalogues, reports, membership lists, and clippings concerning the society preserved in the Henry Lewis Johnson collection deposited in the Dartmouth College Library.

[32] The developing relation between art and printing was cogently stated by John Cotton Dana (1856–1929), amateur Vermont printer and librarian of the Free Public Library of Newark, in *Art Education* for May 1900: 'All of the library's printing, if means and opportunity permit (and the cheapest of printing can show good taste to some ex-

was spied out and settled he began yearning for a new frontier. This time it was a new magazine, an art magazine specifically devoted to printing.[33] The prospectus, typewritten in blue and rubricated, that he carried round among the leading printing houses in 1902, proposed 'The Printing Art: An Illustrated Monthly Magazine. ... As the title indicates, it will be devoted primarily to the Art of Printing and will naturally include the Allied Arts of Designing, Illustrating, Engraving, and Binding. The publication will seek to exemplify the various arts represented by examples of progressive work of publishers and printers, as well as exploiting diverse lines of original work. ... As it will consist of much color work and numerous inserts involving great cost, it is planned to gauge the issue to the number of subscriptions received. ...' The prospectus was signed 'The Printing Art Company, Publishers. Boston, Mass.' but the actual publisher that Johnson found turned out to be the old University Press: John Wilson and Son, Inc., of Cambridge. The Wilson family control had been relinquished and the Whites took over (just in time to force the liquidation of Stone & Kimball in

tent) should be done with a view to its possible influence on design in general and on good printing in particular. Not many people as yet appreciate the fact that the simplest piece of printing is, or may be, either good or bad in design. Few printers consider this at all. The library can do much to attract attention to this subject by giving attention to its printing.' His position was reinforced by George French, author of *Printing in Relation to Graphic Art,* 1903, cited by Dana in his tract *The Art of Printing* (Newark, 1904). This tract described 'an exhibition of the tools, materials, and products of the art of printing' which opened at Newark on January 25, 1904, and was widely influential. Both Dana and French made common cause with Johnson throughout their lives.

[33] Johnson was an inveterate projector of new magazines whenever he was not actually at the helm of one. Promptly after relinquishing the editorship of *The Engraver & Printer* he brought forward a plan for 'Color: A Quarterly Magazine of Color in Typography & Illustration,' of which a dummy for Spring 1896 exists.

1897). The vice-president was William Dana Orcutt and it was with him that Johnson entered into an agreement on December 1, 1902. Under its terms he was to devote his time and energies to the new magazine and to receive a weekly salary. The press assumed the financial responsibilities of publication. Provision was made for the distribution of future profits, but the occasion for payments to Johnson under this clause never arose.

From the first number, which came out in March 1903, *The Printing Art* was better than its promise. Along with articles and discussion, e.g., Rollins on 'Modern "Special" Types,' De Vinne 'About Pages and Margins,' Guido Biagi on 'Jean Grolier: Book-Lover and Patron,' there was a generous showing by means of insets and inserts of excellent work, representing Updike at Merrymount and Rogers at Riverside, the De Vinne and Gilliss presses in New York, Heintzemann with Cornhill Dodgers for Alfred Bartlett, and lively promotional pieces by the Wayside Department of the University Press.[34] Different printing processes were demonstrated in every color of ink on all kinds of papers. The editorial pages kept up meanwhile a discreet but insistent drumming on a favorite theme: printing has been and can be practiced as an art, and it should be so practiced even for reasons of business. Johnson reassured, while he

---

[34] Among exhibitors from New York in the June number is the Cheltenham Press, the pioneer advertising typography firm set up by Ingalls Kimball after dissolution of his partnership with Herbert S. Stone. Kimball was responsible for the Cheltenham typeface design, for which his old friend B. G. Goodhue made the working drawings. The design, originating in 1900–01, was intended for Linotype but before technical problems of production for slug composition had been worked out the American Type Founders Company published it in 1902 — Kimball having sold them the foundry rights reserved under his agreement with Linotype. See Sidney Kramer, *A History of Stone & Kimball and Herbert S. Stone & Co.* (Chicago, 1940), p. 90 f.

stimulated, his audience. 'Art in printing,' he said in the June 1903 number, is not some difficult element from which one is barred by lack of types or other material. . . . There are not many idealists engaged in printing; but to ignore or deprecate artistic endeavor is in the long run fatal to success. . . . To endeavor constantly for a higher standard, and to keep in touch with progressive work in all lines allied to printing, are necessary that the printer may be able to meet the demands of the present. The principles for which *The Printing Art* stands are not visionary nor contrary to the highest business success, but absolutely essential to it.' Tirelessly he expounded this gospel.[35]

[35] His father was the Reverend Albion Henry Johnson. Henry Lewis Johnson (1867–1937) married Mabel A. Wood of Acworth, New Hampshire in 1892. His old friend Henry Lewis Bullen included the following biographical sketch of him in *The Inland Printer* for November 1923:
'I first met my friend Johnson in 1887, when I sold him a printing outfit for the Hyde Park *Times*, of which he was editor. He was born in Limington, Maine, in 1867, the son of a Congregational clergyman. His boyhood was passed in Maine, New Hampshire, California and Massachusetts. He graduated from the English High School in Boston in 1885, where he was the editor of the high school *Record*. Work on the school paper brought him into contact with a good printing house, and determined his career. His first employment was as a reporter on the Boston *Traveler*. In 1887 he bought an interest in the Hyde Park *Times*. At the end of two years, in 1889–91, he took a two-year course in mechanical engineering in the Massachusetts Institute of Technology. In 1897 he organized and was director of the first arts and crafts exhibition in the United States. The arts and crafts movement began in Boston, and Johnson has been active in it from the beginning. In 1891 he became director of printing for the Boston Photogravure Company. Process engraving was then in its infancy, and in 1892 [*sic*] Johnson began publication of the *Engraver and Printer*, which during the five years of its existence surpassed all previous periodicals in its artistry and literary contents. In 1900 he headed a movement which brought about the appointment of the Massachusetts State Commission for Industrial Education. In 1892 [*sic*] he established *The Printing Art*, which under his sole direction for nine years was the indisputable leader among printer's magazines devoted to typographic art and its higher literature. It was a tremendous incentive toward better printing in America. . . .'

The Printing Art immediately became the rallying point for hitherto random effort and latent energies. In the second number, for April 1903, Lindsay Swift of the Boston Public Library had argued the need of constantly reviewing the well-done work of the past in order to balance the new generation's 'unbounded prospects of development, natural, intellectual, and commercial.'

If the printers of to-day, then, do not wish to be esteemed arrogant when they term this calling of theirs an art, they must be willing, and show that they are willing, to subject it to such laws as have made its sister arts so free. All those concerned in what are accepted as the fine arts, the learned sciences, and professions surround themselves with the history, literature, and concrete examples of the work with which they are particularly engaged. Yet it is only in rare instances that such an atmosphere with its material appurtenances is to be found in a printing-office. Art does not flourish in hidden places, nor under restraint, nor in ignorance of what talent and genius have accomplished and are accomplishing throughout the world.[36]

[36] By all accounts the headquarters of Copeland & Day and Alfred Bartlett on Cornhill were full of quaint atmosphere, but Swift would doubtless have rather pointed to Heintzemann's new offices in Dewey Square designed by Goodhue—'a model plant, with reception room and office finished and fitted in the manner of the fifteenth century, plus an ecclesiastical tone, that is very suggestive of the general quality of the service there dispensed' as George French described it in *The American Printer* for May 1901. Updike's careful attention to atmosphere is made clear in his *Notes on the Merrymount Press & Its Work* (Cambridge, 1934).

Swift's own institution, the Boston Public Library, had given the fullest consideration to these matters in the new Copley Square building. Great printers are there architecturally commemorated, with the device of The Riverside Press to represent modern times. Moreover, in producing the *Handbook of the New Public Library in Boston*, 1895, such outstanding bookmen and designers as B. G. Goodhue, Herbert Small, Lindsay Swift, and C. Howard Walker, joined forces to produce a worthy job of printing.

In the March issue of the following year Swift had another article, urging printers to furnish their offices (and minds) with the works of Henri Bouchot, Robert Hoe, Isaiah Thomas, H. R. Plomer, Talbot Baines Reed, William Blades, De Vinne — and so on through a whole page of suggestions. J. M. Bowles wrote, in the May number, about the three important exhibitions recently held by libraries at Newark and New York. 'Lectures or talks on historical, artistic, and technical subjects allied with printing could accompany such exhibits with much profit,' he suggested. And, dwelling mainly on the Newark Free Public Library show, he expressed the hope that 'it may induce a similar movement for the start of collections of various classes of printed matter. . . . Here is the natural home for such collections, for "the library is the printer's debtor."'

The editorial for July 1904 was called 'The Crowning Opportunity of Organization.' It called on printers' groups 'to extend their scope beyond the adjustment of business relations, to the advancement of the art in which they are concerned.' Then following the December editorial this announcement appears:

Notable recognition of the increasing interest in printing is to be found in the action of the Trustees of the Boston Public Library by which a series of public lectures is to be given on the 'History and Art of Printing.' While there are occasional lectures on printing, bookbinding, and allied arts, this series, which is the first of a public character, is suggestive of what can well be undertaken by other libraries and other organizations which may wish to offer similar advantages. The general scope is indicated by the topics which have been announced as follows: December 1st, Type Display in Modern Printing, by Will Bradley; December 15th, Typographical Evolution, by William

Dana Orcutt; January 19th, The Making of Books, by
J. Horace McFarland; January 26th, Symbolism of Form
and Color, by Henry Turner Bailey. Organizations which
include in their membership illustrators, printers, bookbinders, and other craftsmen have opportunities for lectures upon similar topics with much stimulus and profit to
their members and to the public.

The day after Bradley opened the series the *Transcript* reported a large turnout for his lecture, including many illustrators, compositors, lithographers, and
book connoisseurs. The following fortnight's affair
was headlined in the same paper 'The Art of Printing'
and the account continued: 'The second Boston
Public Library lecture in the series on the History
and Art of Printing was delivered last evening by
William Dana Orcutt, head of the University Press at
Cambridge, the subject being "Typographical Evolution."' The speaker, this article went on to say,
stressed the point that good craftsmanship was still
possible and modern conditions afforded opportunities yet ungrasped, but that standards of printing
are regulated finally by the book-buying public.
The rest of the lectures went off as scheduled and the
whole course drew crowds — hundreds of the general
public came to hear talk about printing as an art — to
the frank amazement of a number of the old guard
among Boston printers.

The Boston Public Library lectures generated a
warm enthusiasm for their subject. In this atmosphere
Johnson's suggestion that those most concerned form
an organization to advance printing as an art was
cordially welcomed. Five men were delegated to act
as a 'committee for the formulation of plans for a
society relating to printing,' in Johnson's cautious
language. The members were Updike, Heintzemann,
Rogers, George French, and Johnson. While the

lecture series was still in mid-course the committee met at the University Club on January 10, 1905, to discuss the constitution and form of membership proposal which Johnson had drawn up. The 'printing art club' committee held another meeting at Updike's home on the evening of January 30, and Johnson was able to announce in his editorial pages for February:

A NEW FORM OF ORGANIZATION FOR PRINTERS

While there are strong local and national organizations of printers for trade purposes, there has been heretofore none which exerts any critical, appreciative, or technical supervision, or has had, in any way, to do with the improvement of product. A movement has been started recently in Boston, and a form of organization determined upon, for advancing printing as an art.

It is believed that this new form of organization will be found useful in many centres of printing. Two definite objects are sought:—

The advancement of the standard of work.

The stimulation of the appreciation of printing.

It is anticipated that members of the society will be able to advance the standard of their own work by personal intercourse, by criticism and discussion. A part of the plan is to arrange lectures and exhibitions of printing. Recognition is also to be given to the almost universal public-school instruction in lettering and design. Active and immediate endeavors are to be made to interest educators and librarians in teaching the elements of good printing, and in placing literature and examples bearing upon the subjects within the reach of those concerned.

Another line of effort will be to encourage and influence trade schools in which printing is taught, so as to urge, as far as possible, the adoption of courses of instruction and styles of work approved by the society.

The form of organization is to consist of the usual executive officers and committees on meetings, lectures, exhibitions, and publications. It is not planned to undertake technical instruction, but to serve more as a critical and advisory body.

Printing touches the whole world so intimately that definite knowledge of its underlying principles is of great importance and usefulness, and it is believed that this new organization will do much to advance the standard of product in printing.

By the sixth of February Johnson was ready to send out a call to all those who had signified interest in 'the proposed Society of Printers' to gather and hear the report of their committee. The notices were accompanied by letters from him urging attendance by 'all who have a serious interest in printing' and asking for replies so that he would know how many to count on for dinner.

So on the evening of February 14, 1905, the founders of the Society of Printers first met, broke bread together, adopted a constitution, and elected their governing council for the year. It is impossible to name everyone present on that occasion but, in addition to the five members of the organizing committee, there were almost certainly the other four chosen to make up the nine-man council. The council: Henry Turner Bailey, George French, Carl H. Heintzemann, Henry Lewis Johnson, Frederick D. Nichols, William Dana Orcutt, Bruce Rogers, D. Berkeley Updike, C. Howard Walker. The five-article constitution was handed round in the form of neat page proofs prepared by Updike, using the Caslon type and arrangement which became something of a uniform for the Society's early official printing.

THE SOCIETY OF PRINTERS
BOSTON

. : .

CONSTITUTION

ARTICLE I
NAME

The name of this organization shall be The Society of Printers.

ARTICLE II
PURPOSE

The purpose of this Society shall be the determination and advancement of ideals and standards of printing.

ARTICLE III
GOVERNMENT

1. The government of this Society shall consist of a council of nine members who shall be elected by ballot, a president, vice-president, a secretary and a treasurer being chosen from its number immediately after each annual election.

2. Membership of the Society shall be classed as active and honorary. Active membership shall be limited to fifty of those who are sufficiently interested in the Art of Printing to be of value in advancing the purposes of the Society. Election to active membership shall be by the council. A vote by ballot of three-fourths of the council will be necessary to election. If a candidate fails of an election, he can be proposed again after a lapse of one year. Only active members are eligible to the council.

3. Persons in sympathy with the aims of the Society may be elected to honorary membership by unanimous vote of the council.

4. The name of a candidate for active membership shall be voted upon by the council only after a nomination in writing, proposed and seconded by two members of the Society. The annual fee for active membership is five dollars.

ARTICLE IV
DUTIES OF THE COUNCIL AND OFFICERS

1. The council shall have the power of directors and the immediate government and direction of the affairs of the Society; shall appoint all committees unless the Society in special cases otherwise determines; and make all needful rules and regulations for the government of the Society. It shall have charge of all meetings, lectures, exhibitions and publications and shall make appropriations for the expenditure of funds of the Society. Five members shall constitute a quorum.

2. The duties of the president, vice-president, secretary and treasurer shall be those commonly prescribed.

ARTICLE V
MEETINGS

1. The annual meeting of the Society shall be held on the second Tuesday in November. The council may call or provide for calling a special meeting of the Society at any time, and shall determine the time and place of all meetings.

2. The secretary shall send to each member notice by mail of the time and place of each regular meeting, at least seven days before the same and of the time and place of each special meeting at least four days before the same.

With the addition of a sixth article providing for by-laws and amendments, together with a few trifling changes in punctuation, the constitution was finally approved and adopted as the Society's basic document.

Ten days after the first meeting of the Society the newly elected council convened. On Orcutt's invitation the councilors gathered at the Hotel Empire on Commonwealth Avenue on the evening of February 24 for their initial meeting. They then elected their host first president of the Society. Bruce Rogers was chosen vice-president, Henry Lewis Johnson secretary, and Frederick D. Nichols treasurer. Bailey, who was state supervisor of drawing in the public schools, put the council to work at once on a proposed publication. The project, of which he had prepared a draft, was a manual for the guidance of children in preparing their school papers in pamphlet form, with models for cover designs, title pages, illustrations, sample bindings, etc. 'The Pamphlet' was destined to occupy the attention of many future meetings as well.[37]

At the same time Bailey was busily designing a 'monogram' or device for the Society. It was in demand for the stationery which Updike — who with Rogers and Johnson constituted the standing committee on printing — had in hand. However, when the new stationery was turned out at the Merrymount Press in April and delivered to Johnson in time for his announcement of the Society's May meeting, the nicely drawn S·P in a red field at the head was the design of Bruce Rogers. And there, as official emblem, it has remained to this day, with only a few aberrations from the true way.[38]

[37] The project was finally disposed of at the council meeting November 26, 1912. The committee on printing, headed by Robert Seaver, then reported that the manuscript — by this time representing the work of divers hands — 'as a whole requires a good deal of editing.' Their recommendation of abandoning 'The Pamphlet' and returning the contributed articles to their authors was accepted.

[38] The original drawing has not been located but Rogers redrew the device for the use of the Fortieth Anniversary History Committee in 1945. It is this redrawing of the original which is used as the present model. Walt Harris drew a decorated version which was used on keep-

The May announcement, so dignified, was of Otto Fleischner's talk about a bibliography of printing which the Society proposed to publish listing the books in three major local collections devoted to this subject. Fleischner, assistant librarian of the Boston Public Library, was encouraged to proceed with this useful compilation of works on printing in his library, the Athenæum, and Harvard. It was published the following year, not in the name of the Society but as the Boston Public Library's contribution to the Franklin bicentenary.[39]

The first publication of the Society was a twelve-page pamphlet to serve as official handbook.[40] It came out in June, produced at the Merrymount Press, and with modest but very worthy demeanor communicates a brief history of the Society's origins, its

sakes early in 1915. Another variant appeared first on the title page of the Society's publication *A Keepsake*, 1940 (number XVI of the bibliographical list, Chapter III) and was frequently used for stationery and other official printing. The council of the Society, meeting on May 28, 1942, voted, however, that henceforth 'all the printing of the Society carry the original square seal and not the one with decorative sides, used recently.'

[39] *A List of Books on the History and Art of Printing and Some Related Subjects in the Public Library of the City of Boston and the Libraries of Harvard College and the Boston Athenaeum*. Published in commemoration of the two hundredth anniversary of the birth of Benjamin Franklin. Boston. Published by the Trustees of the Public Library. 1906. There are thirty-eight pages of the bibliographical list followed by fifteen of Franklin portrait reproductions and other plates.

[40] This is number 232 in Julian Pearce Smith's bibliography appended to Updike's *Notes on the Merrymount Press*. Smith does not mention the issue having on the eleventh page: PRINTED FOR THE SOCIETY/JUNE MDCCCCV. (For details of this and subsequent publications of the Society of Printers see the bibliographical list and notes in Chapter III.) In an editorial 'About "Type Revivals"' in his *New England Printer* for January 1936, Johnson reminisced: 'I was once upon a committee with Mr. Updike and Mr. Rogers to produce the first publication of The Society of Printers, Boston. After discussing the various fine types of the Riverside Press, Cambridge, and of The Merrymount Press, Boston, it was decided to print the pamphlet in Caslon Old Style. It still stands as a fine example. . . .'

constitution, and its governing officers. A few lines
of the introduction:

The purposes of the Society are primarily to benefit its
own membership by discussions, by the encouragement of
the study of printing as an art and by interchange of the
results of such endeavors. It is also hoped that through
publications, lectures and exhibitions, an influence will
be exerted for stimulating the general interest in printing
which is already becoming evident.

Besides mentioning the projected bibliography of
books on printing in the vicinity and 'The Pamphlet,'
it speaks of the committee on technical education
whose duty was 'to urge that printing be included in
the courses of instruction given by all organizations
or institutions which have to do with the more important lines of industrial training' and to make
recommendations regarding courses. This committee
was manned by Herbert H. White, W. H. Greeley,
and A. F. Mackay.

The official handbook holds evidence of progress in
the matter touched on in Johnson's notice of the May
meeting, which announced that plans would be made
for the proposed Franklin exhibition in 1906. It also
confirms that plans are under way 'for an exhibition
of printing to be held early in 1906.'

In the two hundredth anniversary of the birth in
Boston of Benjamin Franklin the Society found a
proper occasion for the ambitious exhibition, 'The
Development of Printing as an Art,' which opened at
the Boston Public Library on New Year's Day 1906
and stayed on view for four weeks. The committee
responsible for this achievement took in most of the
membership. Besides those already named as comprising the first council, there were: Arthur Allen,
Winthrop Ames, J. Albert Briggs (who was also the

new treasurer), Theodore Brown Hapgood, Jr.,
Sidney A. Kimber, John Alden Lee, Roger Day
Smith, Edwin T. Stiger, Allen M. Sumner, Lindsay
Swift, and Frederic Allen Whiting. A ninety-four
page handbook was prepared under Stiger's chairmanship which, as *The Printing Art* editorial for March
commented with emphatic redundancy, 'will always
be of permanent value for reference.' The notes cover-
ing early books, bookmaking from 1800 to 1905, paper
and papermaking, and kindred subjects set a model
which for form and content has scarcely been surpassed by anything in its category.[41]

The Library was also the scene of a second series
of public lectures held on five Thursday evenings
between January 4 and April 5 that year. C. Howard
Walker opened with a discussion of 'What Consti-
tutes Style in Printing?' Following this was Lindsay
Swift on 'Benjamin Franklin: the Printer.' Orcutt
spoke on 'Illumination and Its Relation to Book
Decoration.' Bailey's subject was 'Influences for the
Advancement of Printing.' The series ended with
Johnson speaking on 'Decorative Printing.' [42]

Since no secretarial or other official records of
meetings exist for the first three years of the Society,

[41] Smith, in his bibliography in Updike's *Notes on the Merrymount Press*, gives this, the second of the Society's publications, to the Merrymount Press as number 249. Updike himself in the *Notes*, p. 29 f., says: 'In January, 1906, we printed a handbook of an exhibition, *The Development of Printing as an Art*, arranged in honor of the bicentenary of Benjamin Franklin by the Society of Printers of Boston.' However, the man responsible for its production was Edwin T. Stiger of Wilson's University Press and that is doubtless where it was printed.

[42] A similar public lecture series was offered early in 1907. The folder issued for the 1908 season advertises 'Three Illustrated Lectures of Interest to Printers To Be Given at the Boston Public Library' under auspices of the Society of Printers: January 30, 'Modern Printing Establishments and Their Output' by Henry Lewis Johnson; February 27, 'Distinctive Types of American Illustration' by Charles H. Caffin; March 12, 'Design and Color in Printing' by Henry Turner Bailey.

the report in the *Transcript* for March 23, 1906, under
the heading 'Instruction in Printing' is of special
interest. During the meeting at the 4 Joy Street headquarters, the discussion ranged over ground familiar
to readers of *The Printing Art:* plans of the Carnegie
Institute at Pittsburgh, the program of Winona
Technical Institute at Indianapolis, the performance
of the North End Union's Boston School of Printing
as described by Samuel F. Hubbard, the superintendent. The newspaper article concludes:

This educational movement in connection with printing
has already spread to other cities. Twenty-two libraries
and educational institutions have made applications for
the exhibition of the development of the art of printing
recently held under the auspices of this society at the
Boston Public Library. Movements are also under way in
New York and Chicago for similar societies, for the study
and advancement of the art of printing.

The first meeting in the new year of 1906, held on
January 26, had been devoted to Italian printers.
The April meeting, on the twenty-seventh of the
month, featured a talk by Denman W. Ross.[43]
In the way of educating the public about printing,
the crowning effort of the 1907–1908 winter season
was sponsorship of the American visit of the master
of the Doves Press, T. J. Cobden-Sanderson. Orcutt
wrote: 'I arranged lectures for him in New York and
four at Harvard University. The one mentioned in
my diary on December 2 was given under the auspices
of the Society of Printers.' The diary entry for

[43] The first entry in the official record book of the Society opens with
the annual meeting on November 10, 1908. Consequently any notices of
earlier activities depend on other sources. W. D. Orcutt has kindly
transcribed passages from the diary he kept in those years. John Bianchi has placed this history under obligation by making search of the
Merrymount Press files for pertinent correspondence between Updike
and Johnson at the beginning stage of the organization.

December 2, 1907, records that Orcutt 'in p.m. went
to Chickering Hall with Johnson to check on Cobden-
Sanderson lecture on "Book Beautiful". Later called
for Cobden-Sanderson and drove to hall where he
lectured. I introduced him.' [44]

Already, in these early years before the first world
war, the Society's achievements were abundantly ful-
filling its promise. They flowed naturally as the
harvest following wise planting, industrious tillage,
and a fortunate season. The season was fortunate.
Evolutionary forces and the rising standard of living
were taken as laws of a new order. It stood to reason,
under such a benign dispensation, that the printer
most learned in the history of bookmaking and cultivated in the arts relating thereto would also prosper
best. In this atmosphere of hopeful purpose, on its
well-laid foundations, the Society's character was
shaped. Not only the print-fascinated artists and
scholarly bookmen but also practical printers — the
kind who, after hearing reports of the library lecture,
demanded to know what the hell art has to do with
printing — found common ground for rewarding
activities, inspiration, and good fellowship. Unlike

[44] Orcutt's letter to me of May 21, 1945.
For his part, Cobden-Sanderson at 'Hotel Belle Vue' was making his
only journal entry written on American soil:

'. . . In America there is nothing to catch the eye, nothing to fill the
void above the roofs . . . no idea caught from the whole of life and set
up on high, man's mark, his hold upon the infinite. What this should
be I told them — even the Vision; and I told them how the great continent had been withheld from men till man should have attained to the
Vision, that upon the great new continent, unencumbered by the ruins
of the old, and in the great vacancy, the Vision should be enshrined,
and that in the light thereof, as of a new dawn spread backward from
the west to the east, men should walk till all the world should be
within it, and that then "the end should come."

'This has been my message, and yet I have only spoken of Bookbinding and of Printing, of the Doves Bindery and of the Press.' *The Journals of Thomas James Cobden-Sanderson 1879-1922* (London, 1926), II,
98 f.

the conventional social club in which a man's work can be mentioned only with apology, the Society was dedicated from the beginning to shop-talk — but shop-talk at a certain elevation. An eminent and faithful member from early times recently testified that in all the gatherings of the Society he has attended through the years not once has he ever been accosted by a fellow member with something to sell.

The so-called Morris revival was at core the rediscovery by artists that printing offered a proper field for their endeavors (the camera having done its mighty bit toward redefining artistic purposes). The Kelmscott approach was architectonic under all its decoration. Previously the designer with respect to printing had been one who added illustrations or ornamental features to it. Now, in the new light of the 'revival,' the designer could find a place to stand in the printing field analogous to that occupied by the architect in building. Over and over again this was the burden of *The Printing Art*. The printer must know in order that he may express feeling through his collaboration with authors. Feeling was vital to the job: when Updike offered as his stock in trade the attitude of an amateur, along with expert competence, he spoke directly from the root *amare*. Rogers is the lifelong example of the artist specialist who can feel with an author and by typographic means extend his power of expression. The Society soon attracted to its distinguished company others of a feather with these, men like William Addison Dwiggins and Carl Purington Rollins.[45]

[45] Both these men have said that the Society offered them the opportunity of knowing Updike.

Dwiggins came east and settled in Hingham in 1904, shortly after Frederic W. Goudy with whom he had studied in Chicago. Presently he took a studio at 69 Cornhill, Boston, where Alfred Bartlett's publications now gave him much employment as they had once helped

At the very beginning the Society printed 4 Joy Street as its address. For most of its history, however, the organization has been homeless.[46] It has wandered among the hotels, clubs, and restaurants on both banks of the Charles to find places for its meetings. It early commenced cultivating nomadic habits which took the membership further afield at frequent intervals. In 1909 the May meeting was in the form of a pilgrimage to Providence attended by eighteen members. 'The afternoon was devoted to an inspec-

shape his career in Ohio. My review 'Dwiggins As Author,' in *Direct Advertising*, April 1948, contains some notice of this period. About 1910 Rudolph Ruzicka came to Boston to visit Dwiggins and to begin his long association with Updike and Bianchi of the Merrymount Press. Dwiggins also worked for the Craftsman's Guild, of which the moving spirit was Edwin Osgood Grover. Grover, a college classmate of Bartlett (Dartmouth 1894), was the man who had persuaded his shy, club-footed, epileptic friend to make the venture as a publisher 'on a capital of ill health and $75,' and who edited his *Cornhill Booklet* and wrote his first Dodger. An announcement by Grover is reminiscent of the chapbook device employed earlier by Thomas MacKellar to sell old-style types:

Ye Cornhill Printer

I knowe a lyttel *Prynting-Shoppe*	Thys *Prynter* is a luckye man, —
Whose wheels are never still,	Soe often I've hearde tell,
But turne and turne unceasinglye	For every daye he pleasure gets
Att 34 Cornhill.	In doinge all thynges well.

After two more stanzas of this, he concludes:

And I schall claim my lyttel share
In blessings that are his
Because I knewe his work was goode,
And gave him all my Biz.

[46] But see Edward K. Robinson's presidential report for 1923–1924, containing the following: 'Although not strictly connected with the Society, the opening of the new quarters of the Graphic Arts Company at 95 St. James Avenue is of interest to all members of this organization. In the offices of his company, in the exhibition gallery, and in "The Dungeon," Mr. Johnson has virtually created a home for the Society of Printers. May the enterprise live long and prosper!'
In late 1920 and early 1921 meetings were held in Room 18 of the Rogers Building, 'formerly the office of the Institute Secretary but now available as a club room for the Society' according to the record of the February 14, 1921, meeting.

tion of some of the art treasures of that city.' And the record in the careful script of the secretary, Charles Chester Lane, continues, 'In the evening a dinner was held at which Mr. Alfred W. Pollard was the chief speaker. (Mr. Pollard was in Providence for the purpose of cataloguing the books in the Annmary Brown Library).' Many more visits of the sort were made to Providence, and to Worcester and Salem as well. That November of 1909 a more ambitious pilgrimage was organized, setting a pattern for later trips to the New York area also. The members went the rounds of public and private collections including those of J. Pierpont Morgan and George A. Plimpton, John Cotton Dana's Newark Free Library, and Henry Lewis Bullen's newly established library of the American Type Founders Company at Jersey City. The touring Bostonians were given lunch at the Metropolitan Museum of Art and a welcoming delegation of Grolier Club members met them for dinner at The Players.[47] Earlier in the autumn the council had prepared the way by electing several New Yorkers to membership.

The Society's broadening grasp was reflected in the revision of the constitution adopted at the January 1913 meeting. The third article was redrawn to permit the election of men 'living outside the state of Massachusetts who are in sympathy with the aims of the Society' as non-resident members, in addition to the fifty resident (formerly called active) members. A democratizing change in the government provided for the election of officers at the annual meeting of the Society instead of by the council.[48] A step toward

[47] The souvenir menu for this dinner, preserved in Updike's collection at the Providence Public Library, contains autographs of twenty-two guests. See the reproduction, plate 5, herein.

[48] At the council meeting November 13, 1912, Updike was elected to succeed Johnson as president. At the same time he, Robert Seaver,

encouraging publication was taken in the adoption of a new by-law:

An annual report by the president and treasurer shall be printed each year and sent to all members of the Society. In the discretion of the council one or more of the papers delivered before the Society during the year may be printed with this report.

The report for the year 1912–1913 of the president and treasurer, with constitution and by-laws and list of members, printed at the Merrymount Press in the spring of 1914, set an excellent exemplar which, however, was not emulated. Except for the list of members for 1916–1917, under the Whitmarsh administration, a full decade went by with this by-law unheeded. The constitution was substantially overhauled then and the by-law brought into realistic conformity with the facts as follows:

Reports from the president and treasurer shall be submitted each year at the annual meeting. At the discretion of the council, any of the papers delivered before the Society, or the reports of the president and treasurer, may be printed.

Other changes effected by the 1924 revision included a restatement of purpose as the 'study and advancement of the art of printing' (the simpler form used

and C. C. Lane were constituted a committee to draft changes in the constitution. Their work was adopted by the Society on January 29, 1913. The next constitutional revision was carried through in 1924, when the statement of purpose was changed to 'study and advancement of the art of printing,' the permissible resident membership enlarged to seventy-five, and the annual meeting moved from November to May.

In February 1944, as a means of filling the ranks depleted by members absent in the armed services, who were excused from paying dues, an amendment was passed temporarily raising the limit of resident members by the number of those in the service.

on official printing from the outset), enlargement of the permissible resident membership from fifty to seventy-five, and transfer of the annual meeting from November to May. The circumstances are described in the report of the president, Edward K. Robinson, for the year 1923–1924: 'During the year a committee consisting of Messrs. [Irving K.] Annable, Getchell and Iorio was appointed to draft changes in the constitution. This committee reported that Mr. Getchell, after a careful study of the existing constitution and the proposed changes, had rewritten the constitution so that it embodied the suggested alterations and fitted better the present conditions under which the Society operates . . .' The constitution as adopted at the April 1924 meeting is that in present use except for the amendment favorably voted in October 1948 providing for an additional class of membership. All 'those who have maintained continuous resident membership for a period of twenty years' are hereby elevated to senior resident membership. They continue to enjoy the same privileges and pay the same dues as regular resident members but are relieved from the moral obligation to attend faithfully the meetings and actively to support the program of the Society. Their places — about fifteen vacancies resulted from their elevation in the first instance — in the ranks of the resident members are to be filled by younger, fresher troops.

Although the Society did not take up the plan of an annual publication, it did, during Updike's presidency, vote to publish the Cleland talk of April 1913. This was eventually printed and distributed as *Giambattista Bodoni of Parma*. For details of the publications, reference is made to the bibliographical catalogue in the next chapter. The considerable product of an Updike suggestion of the same period, the series of souvenirs or keepsakes, is also dealt with in Chapter III.[49]

A project in which Updike played a leading part was the Harvard course in printing. Its genesis was in *The Printing Art* discussions of education. J. Horace McFarland was a constant and eloquent advocate of training printers for their profession as architects are prepared for theirs. On one of his frequent visits to Boston, he presented his arguments at the January 1910 meeting of the Society to such effect that Dean Edwin F. Gay of the Harvard Graduate School of Business Administration, present as a guest, said he was ready to coöperate with the Society by offering such a course. After talking the matter over generally the meeting voted to have the president appoint a committee to draw up an outline of the proposed course. By the March meeting the committee was ready to report. Besides organizing the course material and arranging for the lectures, there were problems of financing the project and of recruiting qualified students for it which the Society had to consider. No specific record of action in these respects is to be found but before the university opened in the autumn the course had been arranged. It was a two-year program of study offered by the Graduate School of Business Administration for men intending to enter the printing business, under the title 'An Introduction to the Technique of Printing,' consisting of a course of lectures by various specialists, readings, and laboratory work. Many years after, Updike recalled the trepidation with which he went over to Cambridge

---

[49] Beginning with the Fleischner bibliography of selected books on printing and allied interests, the Society has provided the stimulus, encouragement, or occasion for many valuable studies which it did not publish, e.g., J. H. Benton's *John Baskerville*. Many more remain unpublished, e.g., the work by Dwiggins on Caslon ornaments. See note 58.

to give his first lecture that fall. None of this can be discerned in the clear and forceful statement he prepared for the March 1911 meeting of the Society on the subject of the Harvard course. He said, in part:

This course in printing would probably never have existed if it had not been for the enthusiasm and far-sightedness of the members of this Society, of whom I think Mr. Wheelwright and Mr. Johnson should be especially mentioned. . . .[50]

Explaining that he now had to speak for the course, to make up for his sins of omission in the beginning when he had been nothing but cold-water-pourer on the project, he went on seriously:

. . . I think it is 'up to' the Society of Printers, and each member of the Society of Printers, to show his faith by his works in this particular matter, to put his hand in his pocket toward the support of the scheme, and to approach persons outside of the Society who are interested in printing and who might also be willing to give. Such of us as are members of the Society and who are also giving talks in the course must naturally ask for subscriptions, not as teachers in the course, but as members of this Society. So, I speak to you as a member of the Society of Printers and not as a man who happened to be selected to do anything in connection with the course itself. I think it is a matter in which it is important for the Society to show its active cooperation. So far we have urged the course; but we have not supplied the scholars; we have not supplied the money. I do not think we care to remain in this quiescent and admiring condition. . . .

[50] The advisory committee for the course consisted of J. Horace McFarland, T. E. Donnelley, George P. Winship, Amor Hollingsworth, E. B. Hackett, Donald Scott, H. L. Johnson, C. C. Lane, and D. B. Updike. Updike, Johnson, and Hackett were the subcommittee delegated to obtain the Society's help 'to maintain and develop the work along the admirable lines already undertaken.' The estimated expense of the course was between $2,500 and $3,000 a year.

With his appeal, which was printed at the Merry-mount Press at a cost to the Society of $137.56, Up-dike included 'Mr. C. C. Lane's Description of the Course on Printing.' The four-page circular was accompanied by an outline of the Harvard course. Said the 'Description' in part:

In the first year the student takes a course in the history of the printed book, in which the work of the early printers is studied from the historical and artistic viewpoint; a course in the technique of printing, consisting of a series of practical lectures by various specialists . . . ; and courses in accounting, industrial organization, commercial resources, and commercial law.

The four months following this college year are spent in a printing-office, and the student then comes back to the school for his last year of instruction.

The work of the second year consists of an advanced course in the technique of printing, in which a number of practical problems are worked out under close supervision. The instruction is largely in the nature of laboratory work. The student is given practice in laying out copy for the printer, and through various experiments has a chance to work out for himself some of the underlying principles of design and harmony in type forms. He is then required to follow several jobs through the press. . . .

Members of the Society were given a taste of the course at the following January meeting when Updike addressed them on 'Some Early Industrial Conditions and Their Effect upon Typography.' In substance it was one of the lectures he had prepared for the Harvard series. Since students of the course were accorded special memberships in the Society they had the opportunity of hearing this lecture at least twice. Meanwhile the regular members were moved to make some financial contributions to the course.[51]

[51] According to letters in the Updike scrapbook, Merrymount Collection XVII, the Harvard treasurer acknowledged gifts toward the sup-

From the vigorous leadership of the Society's important educational project, the next step, to its presidency, was a natural one for Updike to take. Elected in November 1912, he was continued in the office for a second term and was succeeded only when he declined to be nominated again at the 1914 annual meeting. The Harvard printing course was given up as the country came deeply into the shadow of the first world war but the good results of that effort would be impossible to calculate. Certainly not least was Updike's great *Printing Types*, which had its origins in the lectures he prepared in connection with the Harvard program. This was one instance of the Society shining as an example of 'the invisible university.'[52]

port of the course of $212.44 on June 10, 1912; on May 19, 1913, he acknowledged similarly the receipt of $262.53, of which $100 was paid out of the Society's funds and another $100 given by 'one of the members.' Under date of December 14, 1915, the council again appropriated the sum of $100 for this purpose.

[52] An ambitious educational project is described in the report of Irving K. Annable as president, for the year 1925–1926, although the Society as such was hardly involved:

'Dr. Stratton, President of the Massachusetts Institute of Technology recently expressed his interest in starting a course in printing and allied trades at the Institute. He invited a committee of twenty-four men from the printing and allied trades, coming from all parts of the country, to meet with him on Tuesday, May 11, to confer on the subject. Of these twenty-four men, three were members of this Society. With the approval of Dr. Stratton, your president wrote, in the name of the Society, inviting the committee to meet at the Art Club on the afternoon of May 10 for a preliminary conference, so that the subject could be discussed and ideas formulated to present to Dr. Stratton on Tuesday. The committee organized with the choice of Henry Lewis Johnson as Chairman and Henry L. Bullen as Secretary, both members of this Society. On Tuesday morning the committee met with Dr. Stratton and presented their views, all of the members heartily approving such a course as they knew Tech would provide. While Dr. Stratton did not give any definite decision at the time, we feel much encouraged in the belief that he will act favorably. This committee keeps up its organization for the purpose of rendering further assistance in the matter.'

An elaborate brochure was prepared under the enthusiastic guidance of Johnson and Bullen and issued in 1927 as *Prospectus of a Project for*

A course of public lectures was offered by the Society in 1924 on the general plan of those which had brought it into being, though contrasting significantly with the earlier series as to subject matter and approach. The suggestion had arisen in the spring of the preceding year. Then at the May meeting an outline was put forward for discussion, following the talk on 'Art in Printing from the Layman's Point of View, and the Trade School' by the state director of art education and principal of the Normal Art School, Royal Bailey Farnum. The speaker immediately offered the hospitality of his school for the proposed series of lectures on typographic design. And the council forthwith placed the project in the experienced hands of Johnson as course leader, which was proper since he had been its chief instigator. The series began on the evening of January 10, 1924, and lectures were given at the Massachusetts Normal Art School at fortnightly intervals until May 1. Harry Lyman Koopman led off with a discussion of 'The Book: An Historical Review.' He was followed by Frederic W. Goudy speaking on 'Fine Printing,' Carl Purington Rollins on 'Layout of Book and Booklet Pages,' Heyworth Campbell on 'Layout of Magazine and Other Illustrated Pages,' J. O. Smith on 'Layout of Space Advertising,' Everett Currier on 'Layout of Announcements, Stationery, and Small Forms,' David B. Hills on 'Visualization of the Advertising Idea,' Thomas M. Cleland on 'The Use of Lettering

Establishing a Department of Graphic Arts Research and Engineering, National in Scope, in Connection with the Massachusetts Institute of Technology for the Benefit of the Printing and Allied Industries. A second title was shorter and more pointed: 'One and a Half Million Dollars Required for the Advancement of the Graphic Arts Industries.' President James R. Killian recently looked through the file of his predecessors and reported that apparently only a small working fund was ever raised for this project, which seems to have originated outside the Institute.

and Decoration with Type,' and finally Henry Lewis Johnson presented a summary and review together with 'much information from his rich store of experience on sources of styles and methods.' The series was attended by more than two hundred fifty subscribers at five dollars apiece and the council, in appreciation of Johnson's handling of the affair, voted him an honorarium of one hundred dollars.[53]

Much of the work of the Society throughout its life has been performed unostentatiously, often anonymously, in support of programs identified more prominently with other organizations. When opportunity has offered for useful coöperation in any project consonant with its purposes, the Society has lent a willing and able hand, without worrying about the credit or jockeying for its place in the sun. So, for example, it furthered the founding of the American Institute of Graphic Arts in 1914 and ever since has served the Boston area as the Institute's *locum tenens*. Johnson promptly and generously backed the A.I.G.A. by means of *The Graphic Arts*, in which he carried on the good work previously borne by *The Printing Art*. With his old friends Arthur S. Allen, Bertram Goodhue, and C. F. Whitmarsh, he was one of the Institute's original committeemen. The New York organization and its activities were liberally salted with names familiar to the Society from the time it mounted at the National Arts Club a contemporary design show in the fall of 1914. Since 1923,

[53] In connection with the question of a war tax on tickets to public lectures sponsored by the Society, the following amendment had been adopted at the April 22, 1920, meeting: 'That no officer or member of this Society be paid a salary or receive any payment for services in any connection with the conduct of the affairs of the Society'. This regulation did not survive the constitutional revision of 1924. One hundred dollars was also paid to Rollins for the special keepsake, *The Caslon Crowd*, which he reprinted for course subscribers from the Montague Press edition of 1915. See bibliographical description, p. 75 f.

when the Fifty Books exhibition was regularly put on the road, the Society, often with its old ally the Boston Public Library, has been a perennial sponsor. This long and cordial relationship was early confirmed at a dinner offered by Institute members on May 25, 1915, at the National Arts Club to those of the Society visiting their city.[54] Another example, closer to home but not of such long standing, is to be found in the pleasant relations between the Society and the Bookbuilders of Boston.

Through individuals, too, the Society has reached out to form ties beyond its regional sphere by conferring honorary memberships. The earliest were personal friends and associates of the Society's founders as well as national leaders: Charles Eliot Norton and Theodore Low De Vinne. The next election of honorary members followed parallel lines: the eminent New York printer Walter Gilliss and the dean of the Harvard Graduate School of Business Administration Edwin F. Gay. Before the Society added to this list of four it had almost reached its twentieth birthday. The honor was dispensed worthily but rather in a heartfelt gesture than by any apparent formula, gratefully rather than expectantly. In all these years only twenty-one honorary memberships have been created. This locution is used advisedly instead of 'members elected.' Actually twenty-three have been elected. Five of them were tapped in 1939 following a suggestion by Updike that the Society's thirty-fifth birthday offered a fit occasion for cele-

[54] The American Institute of Graphic Arts was formed to organize a national exhibition of printing to send to Leipzig for the exposition in 1914. It followed the promotional efforts of Arthur Wiener, exposition agent, in New York. However, the American government withheld support and the project collapsed. The Institute turned then to sponsorship of a contemporary design show in connection with the National Arts Club books of the year exhibition.

brating some of those who were doing most for American printing. The action of the council was published in the list of five names issued in September. In November, however, the list had to be revised: the mysterious brothers Grabhorn had declined honorary membership!

On the whole the Society has been content to serve as a hearth, in Updike's genial figure, round which its own members gather for study and mutual encouragement. In this fashion the first twenty years went by before it began feeling anniversary twinges. At the April 1925 meeting Dwiggins entertained the others with stories of the early days. Another five years passed, the Society had weathered a quarter-century, and someone proposed an Old Timer's Night. As the president Thacher Nelson urged the secretary Maurice Blackmur: 'Come out strong in the notice and say we hope T. B. Hapgood, Henry Lewis Johnson, and some of our quaint old characters will come primed to add their reminiscences to the occasion.' Old Timers' Night was held November 24, 1931, but left no trace of what was done and said. In this reflective mood the council commissioned Updike to print a membership roster and got him to write an introductory note for it. This was neatly turned out at the Merrymount Press late in 1931 and distributed at the beginning of the new year. The introduction, deservedly reprinted time and again in official publications, commands space for repetition here:

Note

The Society of Printers for the Study and Advancement of the Art of Printing was founded in 1705, and, unlike many small societies of this kind, has had a long life and shown amazing vitality. The reason for this is that its programme is one which can never be stale or outmoded.

Had it aimed to do any particular thing, it might have failed or expired in the accomplishment of its aim. But as we can never exhaust all there is to know about printing or pause if we desire to advance it, the Society's objective is as true and fresh to-day as when it was formed nearly thirty years ago. At its meetings, the members have listened to almost every eminent worker employed in the field of American printing and its allied occupations, as well as to distinguished printers of other countries. It has arranged visits to libraries and to private collections of printing. It has published books and pamphlets on printing which are worth having and which would not otherwise have seen the light. It has held exhibitions, and its members have attended exhibitions arranged by other organizations. It has supplied funds for the support of printing courses. But perhaps its most valuable work has been to afford a meeting ground for men interested in printing, and, through this, associations, both business and personal, have been formed that otherwise would never have been made. The study of printing and the improvement of work through study has thus been accomplished in no one way, but in many ways, as experience dictated or opportunity offered. That is the reason why the Society is alive now — very much alive!

With each decade there arise new matters to study, new angles of vision, new methods of advancement and new men to represent and explain them. To provide a forum for all this is what the Society of Printers stood for when it was organized, stands for still, and, it is hoped, will stand for in years to come. Whether this hope be fulfilled depends on its members old and new.

The thirties advanced toward the conventional five hundredth anniversary of the 'invention of printing' at the end of them. Within the Society the awakening historical sense was accompanied by a valetudinarian mood, which grew acute as those whom younger members had learned to think of as patriarchs began to drop off. Henry Lewis Johnson died on December

10, 1937.[55] The following summer Theodore Brown Hapgood died. In announcing the 1939 annual meeting for the last day of May, the retiring president George F. Trenholm called attention to the imminence of the Society's thirty-fifth birthday and

[55] Updike prepared a characteristically unflinching memorial to Henry Lewis Johnson. Signed and dated by him January 24, 1938, it was read at the meeting of the Society on the next evening:

'It is not long ago that death took from the membership of the Society of Printers one of the men who did most to promote its beginning, and who throughout its history has been deeply interested in it — proposing from time to time activities, sometimes wise and sometimes impracticable, which however contributed to its vitality. Some old papers which I was lately looking over, recalled too that this man was also one of the most enthusiastic promoters of the Society of Arts and Crafts, and that the original invitations to organize it were signed by Mr. Charles Eliot Norton and himself. These two societies — the Society of Printers, and the Society of Arts and Crafts — both owe to him much of the spade work done in their behalf in early days. And then too *Printing Art* as in later times *The New England Printer* were due to his initiative. None of these varied activities came to great fruition — to him. When his schemes succeeded, they fell into other hands. When they failed, it was he who generally lost as well — either in money or in influence, for we can "try everything once" except failure!

'The death of this early member of the Society gives us food for thought. His life was not a material success, nor did he himself think so, and it came to an end under circumstances of discouragement, illness and privation. We sit comfortably at this table and perhaps inwardly pray (to paraphrase the Psalmist) that our last end may *not* be like his. For most of us, I do not think that is at all likely. It is not likely because apart from visionary qualities he also had vision — far more than some whose activities have been more effective, prosperous and rewarding. He did "follow the gleam" even though it was sometimes but a will-o-the-wisp, and there was something fine and noble about his persistent efforts to carry on, to do which he tried far harder than most of us think worth while. In short, he faithfully followed the light he saw and he led others to it. And to do that is success.

'It is just because I often was impatient with his plans and because it is easy for us to dismiss him from our thoughts with a sigh — that I have wished to say at a meeting of this Society, words that I am sure we all feel should be said and which are his due. I do not know where the grave is where he lies, but the stone above it might well be inscribed with that ancient phrase — "God is perfection, and he that strives after it is striving for something divine."'

No inscription may mark the grave of Henry Lewis Johnson. With the same devotion to ideals that governed all his life, he gave his body at last to the advancement of science.

pleaded for older members to bring in keepsakes, publications, clippings, and notices. Updike responded by bringing into the meeting the scrapbook he had titled 'Printing Connected with the Society of Printers Boston,' containing the carefully mounted souvenirs of his many years of association, and placing it at the service of any officer designated to set down a permanent record. A past president and historian of printing, David T. Pottinger, suggested that provision be made for gathering historical material into a book, at the fiftieth anniversary or prior dissolution of the Society. To mark the celebration both of the Society's and of Gutenberg's anniversary *A Keepsake ... Being the Address of William Dana Orcutt, Esqr. at the First Meeting of the Society* was printed in May 1940 by D. B. Updike, The Merrymount Press. At the end of 1941 Daniel Berkeley Updike died.

The thirty-fifth anniversary had gathered so much momentum that the fortieth was attended with extraordinary preparations. As a sort of warm-up exercise the 1944 annual meeting was given over to reminiscences led by George Parker Winship, abetted by Carl P. Rollins and George P. Tilton, under the general rubric 'The Past and Future of the Society of Printers and Carl H. Heintzemann, Printer.' The council in June created the Fortieth Anniversary History Committee charged with gathering materials for an exhibition and for a chronicle to be prepared for eventual publication.[56] Founders' Day was observed on February 14, 1945, by issuance of a four-page note under that title. On May 9 at the Hotel Lenox the annual meeting as 'Past Presidents Night'

[56] In addition to the brief account of its origins in the first Society publication, of June 1905, there had been only the historical sketch, 'Printing for Its Own Sake,' by Edgar B. Sherrill in the *Transcript* of August 29, 1922.

drew Frank Chouteau Brown, Sidney A. Kimber,
C. C. Lane, William Dana Orcutt, and others of the
Society's incunabula period. After dinner the meeting
adjourned to an exhibition of keepsakes, publications,
and other memorabilia that filled the Treasure Room
cases in the Boston Public Library.[57] Among the
salutes which the anniversary produced from other
organizations was this one signed by Frederick B.
Adams, Jr., as secretary pro tempore of the Grolier
Club council:

The Council of the Grolier Club, at its meeting of
February eighth, requested me to convey their compliments and congratulations to your Society on the occasion
of the celebration of your Fortieth Anniversary, on February fourteenth, nineteen forty-five.
The purposes of your Society evoke a hearty sympathy
from us; you have, over the years, done much to promote
the union between Art and Typography in commercial
as well as 'fine' printing; it is therefore natural that we
should wish you well for the future.

[57] Walt Harris, J. Horace McFarland, Edward K. Robinson, and
George P. Tilton all wrote pleasant tributes in response to the meeting
invitation while excusing themselves from attending.
Besides the Founders' Day note more particularly described in the
next chapter, the present writer published two articles bearing on the
Society's history: 'The Society of Printers and the Public Library' in
More Books (Bulletin of the Boston Public Library) for May 1945, as
cited; 'The Approach to Printing as an Art in America,' De Gulden
Passer, numbers 1–2 (Antwerp, 1947).

III

Fifty Years of Printing as an Art

THE test of a society for the study and advancement of printing as an art is pretty much the same as for a church: the character and performance of its members. In the long run it will be judged not by their public professions of a high-sounding credo but by their success in turning to account in their work what Cobden-Sanderson called (rather hieratically) the Vision. The following pages are devoted to the work of members done in the name of the Society of Printers.

Since printers are used to clarifying their ideas by setting them in type, it is not remarkable that official printing began even before the first meeting of the Society, as a means of settling on proposal forms for the constitution and membership applications. From that time onward, other than replenishing the stationery supply, printing for the Society or in its name falls into two categories: books, circulars, and pamphlets issued as official publications; and souvenirs, keepsakes, announcements, and notices produced in connection with particular meetings or events.

It is clear from the series indication on the Society's second publication that a publishing program, however modest, was contemplated from the beginning. As a matter of fact publication stood first among the means to be employed in promoting printing as an art, as announced in the official handbook at the outset. Nevertheless, the number of works published by the Society throughout its half-century is small; although if all the papers prepared for its meetings and all the studies growing out of its activities, subsequently published elsewhere, were counted, the list might well be worthy of an 'invisible university.' It could be further extended by adding the titles of many books and pamphlets made available to members in a special issue or otherwise, though published primarily for another purpose and audience.[58]

Limited to publications properly attributable to the Society of Printers, the list stands as follows:

I

THE SOCIETY OF PRINTERS | FOR THE STUDY AND ADVANCEMENT OF THE ART OF PRINTING | S·P [device in orange square] BOSTON MASSACHUSETTS | MDCCCCV

[12] pp.; 9 by 5¾ inches; sewn, in blue charcoal paper cover.

Contents: [1] title, [2] blank, [3]–[4] The Society of Printers, [5]–[7] constitution, [8] blank, [9]–[10] officers, council, and committees for mdccccv, [11] printed for the Society June mdccccv, or blank in the variant issue, [12] blank.

[58] Mention has already been made of works growing out of the Society's activities, such as *A List of Books on the History and Art of Printing* (Boston Public Library, 1906), of Benton's *Baskerville*, and Updike's *Printing Types*. Papers prepared for meetings years ago keep proving their vitality by cropping out in print, as for example the Rollins address at the March 1936 meeting which was collected in his volume *Off the Dead Bank* (New York, 1949). Johnson, during his lifetime, published many of the papers delivered before the Society, in his various journals; e.g., Lawrence C. Wroth's 'The Work of the Merrymount Press' was promptly secured and printed in the December 1935 issue of *The New England Printer*.

Among the publications made specially available to members of the Society although prepared primarily for a larger public may be mentioned Pottinger's *Printers and Printing* and Updike's *Some Aspects of Printing Old and New*. Special signed issues respectively of a hundred and of seventy-five copies were made for the Society in 1941.

See page 48 f. of text and note 40 for circumstances of this publication and additional information about it.

II

THE DEVELOPMENT | OF PRINTING AS AN ART | A HANDBOOK | OF THE EXHIBITION IN HONOR OF | THE BI–CENTENARY OF FRANK– | LIN'S BIRTH HELD AT THE | BOSTON PUBLIC LIBRARY | UNDER THE AUSPICES | OF THE SOCIETY | OF PRINTERS | S·P [device in orange square] | PUBLICATIONS OF THE SOCIETY, NUM– BER II | BOSTON, MASSACHUSETTS | JANUARY 1 TO 29, 1906

[vi], 1–94 pp.; 8¾ by 5½ inches; sewn, glued-on cover to match that of first publication.

Contents: [i] half-title, [ii] blank, [iii] title page, [iv] copy-right, [v] officers and council, exhibition committees, [vi] blank, 1–94 catalogue and notes. 'The interest and educational value of the exhibits will be greatly strength-ened by following them with this Handbook, which con-tains a running synopsis . . .'

See page 49 f., also note 41. Although accepted by Updike himself, this production is erroneously ascribed to the Merrymount Press by Smith in his bibliography.

III

[Harvard course in printing: an appeal by D. B. Updike and description by C. C. Lane, presented at the annual meeting of the Society on March 8, 1911.]

[4] pp.; 11 by 8½ inches.

For contents of this circular printed at the Merrymount Press see page 59 f.

IV

THE SOCIETY OF PRINTERS | FOR THE STUDY AND ADVANCEMENT OF | THE ART OF PRINT– ING | S·P [device in orange square] | REPORTS OF THE

PRESIDENT AND TREASURER | WITH CON-
STITUTION BY–LAWS | AND LIST OF MEMBERS |
BOSTON MASSACHUSETTS | MDCCCCXIV
[16] pp.; 9 by 5¾ inches; sewn pamphlet, in green wrapper.
Contents: [1] title page, [2] blank, [3]–[6] president's
report 1912–1913 signed D. B. Updike, November 1913,
with his additional note dated March 1914, [7] treasurer's
report, [8]–[9] officers, council, committees, [10]–[13] constitution and by-laws, [14]–[15] list of members, [16]
imprint: The Merrymount Press Boston.

V

[Roster, 1915]
This item has been seen only in galley proof form, headed
SOCIETY OF PRINTERS | 1915, and containing the
following classifications: officers, council, committees,
resident members, non-resident members, honorary members, and student members (of the last none is listed.)

VI

[Roster, 1915–1916]
Like the foregoing entry, this has been seen only in galley
proof, headed SOCIETY OF PRINTERS | 1915–1916,
with classifications as before except that the final class is
changed to: students in printing course, with twelve
names.

VII

SOCIETY OF PRINTERS | 1916–1917
[4] pp.; 8½ by 5 inches.
Contents: [1] heading as given followed by officers, council,
and beginning of resident members, [2] continuation resident members, [3] non-resident and honorary members,
[4] student members, of whom ten are listed.
   The typography of this circular matches the two preceding rosters. The printer was doubtless Getchell.

VIII

GIAMBATTISTA BODONI | OF PARMA | T. M. CLE-
LAND | S·P [device] | Boston | THE SOCIETY OF
PRINTERS | MCMXVI
[6], 7–50 pp.; 9 by 6 inches; bound in terra cotta paper-
covered boards.
Contents: [1] half-title, [2] certificate: two hundred and
fifty copies printed by The University Press, [3] blank,
[4] portrait: monument to Bodoni at Saluzzo, [5] title
page, [6] copyright by Cleland, 7–50 text of address and
biographical sketch of Bodoni.
The address had been delivered at the April 22, 1913,
meeting of the Society. The publication committee's announcement of its completion is dated December 30,
1916.[59]

IX

PUBLIC LIBRARY OF THE | CITY OF BOSTON | AN
INSPIRATION | IN ITS ARCHITECTURE, SCULP-
TURE, AND | MURALS, AND A GREAT RE-
SOURCE | FOR THE STUDY OF THE ART | AND
TECHNIQUE OF | PRINTING | *With a Selected List of* |
Books on Printing | S·P [device] | BOSTON | SOCIETY
OF PRINTERS | 1924
[4], 5–15, [1] pp.; 8¼ by 5¼ inches; wire-stitched, self-
covered.
Contents: [1] title, framed by thick-thin rule, [2] blank,
[3] preface signed Society of Printers, [4] blank, 5–14 text

[59] Hans Mardersteig of the Officina Bodoni spoke to the Society at
the October 15, 1936 meeting. On November 10 he wrote from Verona
to the secretary: 'On the evening of my visit your President very kindly
offered me a book as a souvenir of the occasion. I did not open the
parcel until I was on the way back to New York, and then, to my
surprise and pleasure, I found that it was a copy of Mr. Cleland's
study of Giambattista Bodoni, a book of which I had already heard,
but which I had never had a chance of seeing. Will you please convey
my thanks to the members of your Society for this most appropriate
gift, and tell them and Mr. Cleland that I could not resist reading the
book right through the same night. I consider it an admirable account
of Bodoni's life and work.'

and list of books, 15 note signed Henry Lewis Johnson, [16] blank.

According to the prefatory note, 'The immediate occasion for this publication has been the course in Typographic Expression at the Massachusetts Normal Art School in the Spring of 1924.' The book list, with call numbers, occupies seven pages; it is divided under the following subject headings: Historical, Technical, Design and Lettering, Bookbindings, Type Specimens, Engraving, Printers' Devices, Famous Presses.[60]

Another piece issued in connection with the same course of lectures qualifies as a publication of the Society:

X

THE | CASLON | CROWD | *Being a Slight Disquisition,* | *with Exemplifications, on* | *that Typographical Para-* | *gon, the Caslon Letter.* | [Chorobates Press mark in panel] | Set up for the *Society of Printers* by | Carl Purington Rollins. Printed | at Yale University Press, New | Haven, Connecticut, 1924. | [fleuron border]
[8] pp.; 7¼ by 4 inches; sewn pamphlet, in grey-blue printed wrapper.
Contents: front cover, title as given, [1]–[6] text of The Caslon Crowd and bibliographical note as follows: 'Being still a willing member of the Caslon Crowd, despite the revivification of Garamond, of Bodoni, and of Baskerville,

---

[60] The idea and execution of this publication were no doubt Johnson's. Long a member of the Boston Public Library's Examining Committee, of which Updike later became a member with him, he was constantly calling to the attention of printers the riches of that Library. He frequently published articles about it in his journals and within a year or so of the time of his death was actively working on a monograph relating to its special collections and trust funds.

The most commanding production called forth by the lecture series was a folio reproduction of a page from the Forty-two Line Bible with an accompanying note in blackletter by Harry Lyman Koopman. It was printed at The Riverside Press under the direction of G. P. Winship and Anselmo Bianchi and presented in behalf of the Society to those attending the first lecture. The archives show that many years later an earnest printing instructor hunted high and low for a copy of this piece but could come by none.

I am glad to reprint, with a few changes, this bibelot which I issued from the Montague Press in the year 1916. C. P. R.,' [7] Caslon alphabet, [8] blank.

In spite of the statement of the author-printer, the Montague edition is plainly dated 1915. See page 62 f. and note 53 for the circumstances of this publication.

XI

THE SOCIETY OF | PRINTERS | [rule] | *For the Study | & | Advancement of the | Art of Printing* | [rule] | LIST OF MEMBERS | 1930–1931 | [rule] | BOSTON: MDCCCCXXXI | [ornamental frame, decorations at head and foot]
[ii], 1–9 pp.; 5½ by 3¼ inches; wire-stitched, self-covered. Contents: [i] title, [ii] imprint, The Merrymount Press, Boston, 1–2 note signed D. B. Updike, 3–9 list of members, [10] blank.

The text of Updike's note is given on page 65 f.

XII

WOOD ENGRAVING | AND | WOOD ENGRAV-ERS | BY HIRAM CAMPBELL MERRILL, SC.
15, [1] pp., 2 leaves; 10¾ by 8 inches; punched and laced, in printed brownish-red wrapper.
Contents: frontispiece reproduction of Merrill wood-engraving after Schell; 1 title and beginning of text, 2–13 text, 14 blank, 15–[16] publication note; between pages 8 and 9 is Merrill's signed portrait.

The copyright is 1937 by the Society of Printers. Five hundred copies were printed by Gordon-Taylor Inc. at the Abbey Press.[61]

[61] As early as 1911 there had been an exposition of the wood-engraver's craft before the Society by Frank French. Timothy Cole spoke to members in the spring of 1916 and in 1932 they saw his film 'Last of the Wood-engravers.' The Merrill meeting at which the present paper was delivered was held in January 1937.

XIII

LIST | OF MEMBERS | 1937–1938 | [panel, S·P device in red square] | A NOTE | PAST OFFICERS | CON-STITUTION & BY–LAWS | OFFICERS & COUNCIL | 1937–1938 | [rule] | THE | SOCIETY OF PRINTERS | BOSTON | [frame, star-and-rule ornament at head and foot]

[1], 2–24, [1] pp.; 5⅜ by 3½ inches; bound in pink paper-covered boards.

Contents: [1] title, 2–3 note by Updike, 4–11 past officers, 12–16 constitution and by-laws, 17 officers & council, 18–24 list of members, [25] acknowledgment of contributions.

XIV

LIST | OF MEMBERS | 1939–1940 | [panel with S·P device in red square] | THE | SOCIETY OF PRINTERS | BOSTON | [frame, star-and-rule ornament at head and foot as before]

[12] pp.; 5⅜ by 3⅜ inches; wire-stitched, self-covered.

Contents: [1] title page, [2] blank, [3] officers & council, [4] blank, [5]–[11] list of members classed as resident, non-resident, and honorary, [12] blank.

The treasurer's report dated May 1, 1939, included a payment of $74 for 'Constitution and Roster.' Since none has been seen for that administrative year, i.e., 1938–1939, it is not clear to which year the bill belongs.

XV

LIST | OF MEMBERS | 1940–1941 | ...
The format and contents are the same as in the preceding item.

XVI

SP [device in red tablet] | A KEEPSAKE | printed in the year of the | Five Hundredth Anniversary of the | IN-VENTION OF PRINTING | and Commemorating the thirty-fifth year | since the Inauguration of | THE SOCIETY OF PRINTERS | Being the Address of | *WILLIAM DANA ORCUTT, Esqr.* | at the First Meeting of the Society | February 24, 1905 | [thin-thick rule; rubricated]

[vii], viii, [1], 2–7, [1]; 6¾ by 4¼ inches; bound in marbled cloth.

Contents: [1] half-title, [ii] blank, [iii] title page, [iv] blank, [v] officers and council for 1939–1940, [vi] blank, [vii]–viii foreword signed W. C. A[llen], [1]–7 address by Orcutt, [8] colophon.

Three hundred copies arranged and printed by D. B. Updike, The Merrymount Press, May 1940. The expense of the 'thirty-fifth anniversary book' appears in the May 1941 treasurer's report as $214. The title page is in error.[62]

XVII

THE SOCIETY [S·P device in red square] OF PRINTERS | A Testimonial Dinner | to | WILLIAM DANA ORCUTT | Book Designer and Typographer | First

[62] Orcutt was elected president by his fellow members of the council at the first council meeting on February 24. This followed by an interval of ten days the first meeting of the Society, which had elected the council. The record was set straight in the note on Founders' Day distributed at the fortieth annual meeting of the Society on February 14, 1945. See p. 44, p. 47, p. 68, and number XX of this bibliographical catalogue.

In response to a question raised on the 1940 Keepsake regarding this point, Orcutt wrote me on January 15, 1945, quoting from his old day-by-day diary the following entries. The accompanying comments are his.

'February 14, 1905 — "Dinner of Society of Printers at Victoria to elect council, of which I was one." This was the first step in the formation. 'February 24, 1905 — "Council of Society of Printers met at 333 Commonwealth Avenue in the evening and elected officers. W.D.O., President; Bruce Rogers, Vice-President; Nichols, Treasurer; H. L. Johnson, Secretary." This is the meeting at which I made the remarks which were perpetuated in the Keepsake printed by Mr. Updike. . . . My remarks at the council meeting, which were glorified by being printed by Mr. Updike, were not intended as an address but as a statement of my personal approach to the idea of forming a Society such as was contemplated. Other members of the council also made remarks at the time. This was before the voting for officers. . . .'

President of the Society of Printers | who, on | November 3,
1941, celebrated his | 50th Anniversary in the Graphic
Arts | [ornament] | In recognition of his unprecedented
continuous | service and distinguished contributions to
the | Art of Printing, we pay him tribute | [ornament] |
FRIDAY, FEBRUARY 13, 1942 | Dinner at Six-
Thirty P. M. | SCHRAFFT'S WEST STREET BOS-
TON | *Composed in Mr. Orcutt's Laurentian type* [within
square brackets]
[10], 11–34 pp.; 10½ by 8¼ inches; bound in blue cloth.
Contents: [1] half-title, [2] 'Arranged and printed at the
Plimpton Press. Limited to 200 copies of which 100 are for
the Society of Printers and 100 for friends of the Plimpton
Press,' [3] title page, [4] blank, [5] half-title, [6] blank,
[7] remarks by president, [8] blank, [9] half-title, [10] blank,
11–12 introduction by Herbert Farrier, 13 half-title,
[14] blank, 15–34 remarks by Orcutt.

XVIII

Membership Roster of | the Society of Printers | S·P
[device in black square] | Boston, Massachusetts | 1943–
1944
[12] pp.; 5½ by 3⅜ inches; wire-stitched, in printed wrapper.
Contents: [1] title, [2] blank, [3] officers and council,
[4] blank, [5]–[10] resident members, [10]–[11] non-resident
members, [11]–[12] honorary members.

The display composition is in Goudy Text.

XIX

SOCIETY OF PRINTERS | *MISCELLANY* | S·P
[device in square] | A CO–OPERATIVE VENTURE IN
WARTIME PRINTING | PRODUCED BY MEM-
BERS | FOR PRIVATE DISTRIBUTION TO THE
SOCIETY | [ornament] | SOCIETY OF PRINTERS·
BOSTON | 1945[63]

[63] The *Miscellany* had been heralded by a circular sent out to members in September 1943. 'Shall the members of the Society print a

12 unnumbered preliminary pages, 44 leaves comprising fifteen sections; 9¼ by 6⅛ inches; decorated paper-covered boards, pasted label.

Contents: [1] half-title, [2] blank, [3] title page, [4] copyright, [5] contents, [6] blank, [7]–[9] foreword signed **Ray Nash**, [10] chairman's note signed G. F. T[renholm], [11] contributors and credits,[12] blank; the contributed sections: [a] 'The First Printing at Randall Hall' by Carl Rollins, printed by Harvard University Printing Office, [b] 'Brother Jeromy: Afterpiece for Marionettes' by W. A. Dwiggins and with his illustrations, printed by G. Gehman Taylor and Millard D. Taylor at their private press in Stoneham, [c] 'The Four Beliefs' by Robert Frost with a wood-engraving by J. J. Lankes, printed at the Graphic Arts Workshop, Dartmouth College, [d] '"By J. Johnson Printer,"' prepared by Carl G. Smith and printed at the Athenæum Press, [e] 'John Baskerville's Type in America' by Paul A. Bennett, designed and printed by Fred Anthoensen, [f] 'The Tramp Printer: the story of T. P. James, who stopped at Brattleboro long enough to be the Spirit Pen of Charles Dickens' from *The Annals of Brattleboro*, designed and printed by Robert L. Dothard at E. L. Hildreth & Company, [g] 'A woodcut of the old Ebenezer Hubbard House Concord, Massachusetts' engraved by Philip Conant Holden and with his note on it, [h] 'The Book Beautiful: T. J. Cobden-Sanderson' designed by William Dana Orcutt and printed at the Plimpton Press, [i] 'S·P Papermakers privileged to mix among their betters . . .' by Herbert Farrier, Amor Hol-

book?' it inquired, and proceeded with an affirmative argument. At the end of the following January, the chairman of the committee, George F. Trenholm, answered the question with a rousing 'Yes! The Members of the Society of Printers will print a book,' and in this second circular called for contributions of signatures from members. 'The Council of the Society will act as Publication Committee. They look forward to issuing for you, a book worthy of our history and unique in our activities. Its production challenges our loyalty to our principles and our regard for our founders. . . . Printers have always produced — in good times and in bad — in war and in peace. Let us hold to our heritage as a Society of Printers.'

lingsworth, Jr., and Howard Wallingford, printed by Donald Hagar at his Rapid Service Press, [j] 'Where's That Proof? or, a glimpse of the printing industry, Boston 1854' drawn by Raymond Lufkin fondly and nostalgically, [k] 'The Atlantic Charter' designed and printed by Walter W. Annable at the Berkeley Press, [l] 'From the First Inaugural Address of Thomas Jefferson' produced by Forrest Orr, Richard Robertson, and Arthur Williams, [m] 'How do Roses get into Print?' by J. Horace McFarland, illustrated with his photographs and printed at his Mount Pleasant Press, [n] 'New Hampshire, Land of Scenic Splendor,' four-color process print contributed by Carlton M. Strong and Harry M. Faunce of the Rumford Press, [o] 'Time . . . A Boy Died Last Night,' decorated by Ronald W. Murray, arranged and composed by Frank Lightbown and printed by Albert R. Getchell.

The list of contents inadvertently omits the section designated [h] in the present listing.

XX

S·P [device in orange square] | THE SOCIETY OF PRINTERS: FOR THE STUDY AND | ADVANCE-MENT OF THE ART OF PRINTING: BOSTON | ˙.˙ | FOUNDERS' DAY
[4] pp.; 9 by 6 inches.

'The foregoing note on Founders' Day is condensed from the fortieth anniversary history of the Society in preparation by our committee. . . .' Signed Ray Nash, it was prepared for distribution at the meeting of the Society on February 14, 1945, the fortieth anniversary day of founding.

XXI

THE WORK OF | Carl Purington Rollins | CPR [calligraphic ornament] | Arranged and presented by THE SOCIETY OF | PRINTERS, Boston and exhibited at the First | Corps Cadet Armory on Columbus Avenue, | in

Boston, during the 950 PRINTING AND | PUBLISHING WEEK, January 6TH *to* 9TH | [frame; rubrication]
[2], 3–5, [1] pp.; 8⅛ by 5¾ inches; wire-stitched, self-covered.
Contents: [1] title, [2] blank, 3–4 Rollins Revisited, by Peter Beilenson, reprinted from the *Journal* of the A.I.G.A., 4–7 by Bruce Rogers, reprinted from the catalogue of 'A Half-Century of Work and Play with Type,' an exhibition arranged by the class in graphic arts and displayed in the Baker Library, Dartmouth College, [8] officers and council.

XXII

LIST OF MEMBERS | 1950–1951 | [panel] | S·P [in red square] | A NOTE | PAST OFFICERS | CONSTITUTION & BY–LAWS | OFFICERS & COUNCIL 1950–51 | Founded 1905 | [below panel] THE SOCIETY OF PRINTERS / *Boston*
[1], 2–31, [1] pp.; 5⅜ by 3⅜ inches; wire-stitched, self-covered.
Contents: [1] title, 2–3 note by Updike written in 1931, 4–14 past officers, 15–21 constitution & by-laws, 22 officers & council, 23–31 list of members classified as senior resident, resident, non-resident, honorary, [32] blank.

XXIII

THE TREND OF THE 50 *of '52* | *An address given by RONALD MURRAY* | *on April 29, 1953, before the Society of Printers on the occasion of the exhibition of the fifty best* | *books printed in 1952, as selected by the American Institute of Graphic Arts*
[16] pp.; 5⅛ by 7¼ inches; wire-stitched, self-covered.
Contents: [1] title, [2]–[15] text of address, [16] imprint of Thomas Todd Company, designed by Ramon Folta.
    This item was sent to members at Christmas 1953 'as a holiday greeting from the president and council of the Society of Printers, but more especially from fellow mem-

bers Ron Murray and Tom Todd Jr., author and printer respectively.'

Some of the Society's abortive publishing projects make a longer tale than those completed. As an egregious example there is the Heintzemann monograph already touched on, a stubborner case even than 'The Pamphlet' (see Chapter II *passim* and note 37) which lasted seven years before it winked out. The monograph project seems to have started at the September 1924 meeting of the Society. The guest of the evening was Carl Rollins who, among brief remarks after dinner, suggested that Carl Heintzemann and his work offered an excellent opportunity for a publication. G. P. Winship moved that a committee be appointed to publish a volume on this subject and he was appointed out of hand as chairman of it. President Robinson appointed H. L. Johnson and D. B. Updike to serve with Winship and, when Updike subsequently begged off, named Edgar B. Sherrill in his stead. David T. Pottinger was also added to the committee.

The official records are silent for years and years. But the existence of the project is revealed — like a drifting hulk lit by a lightning flash — in a letter of the president, John Coolidge Hurd, dated May 31, 1929. The annual meeting had just voted unanimously to publish a book on the Merrymount Press during the ensuing year and Pottinger was now being asked to prepare a monograph on that subject. 'You may ask what has become of the Heintzemann project,' said Hurd. 'This has hung fire for several years and as the Merrymount Press has just completed thirty-five years of existence it seems wise to concentrate all energies on publishing an Updike book. If, in the meantime, you can encourage Fred Mackay to select material for the Heintzemann book it might be a suitable successor to our first effort. . . .' In an account of that 1929 annual meeting the secretary further told of an enthusiastic discussion to the effect that the Society ought to issue some sort of publication; when someone spoke of a small book on Heintzemann, the prevailing sentiment was for the new book on Updike.

Neither monograph progressed, and eventually history began to repeat itself. At a meeting of the Society council, which included Charles the son of Carl Heintzemann, on January 5, 1937: 'Motion was made and seconded that the Society publish a monograph on the Carl Heintzemann Press. Mr. Taylor reported that he had obtained the co-operation of W. A. Dwiggins and T. B. Hapgood in the production of such a book. It was suggested that different people, particularly Carl P. Rollins, be asked to submit material for this work, dealing with different phases of their personal experiences with the Press. This motion was voted, following which an amendment to the motion was passed to the effect that the book be set in 337 Caslon type.' When the council next convened on February 9 the president already had favorable news. Rollins would be editor and Dwiggins would contribute information. At its mid-April meeting the council heard that the material on the Heintzemann Press contributed by H. L. Johnson had been turned over to the editor. The annual meeting of the Society on May 20, 1937, was told that the monograph would be published that year.

There it lodged again. President Taylor cajoled and needled but at last in May of 1938 he had to lay down his gavel without another word on the Heintzemann book. The president's report for the succeeding year, 1938–1939, mentioned the project hopefully. And so it lingered along until the annual meeting on May 11, 1944, when George Parker Winship performed a rite of absolution before the Society, acceptable and sufficient to dispose of the Heintzemann monograph, at least for the time being. His talk, scheduled to be on 'Carl H. Heintzemann, Printer' thus brought to an end (or pause, anyway) twenty years of effort, engaging excellent talents and great loyalty and gratitude, to express appreciation in a simple volume. All this coming to no result shows once more that the printing sort make hard work of writing about themselves, especially when their feelings are involved and they are anxious to make a really nice job of it. Perhaps the project only rests, to rise refreshed another day and fight through to a victorious finish.

The second general category of printing done in the name of the Society comprises the much more numerous output of announcements and meeting notices, souvenirs or keepsakes, dinner menus, and so forth, produced in connection with particular meetings or events. A long series of these pieces had its inception a couple of months after Updike took office as president. At the council meeting of February 3, 1913, according to the old manuscript record book, 'The printing of souvenirs for the meetings of the Society was discussed. It was suggested that each of these souvenirs be the work of a single member. It was further *Voted* that the Treasurer be authorized to make payments, during the current year, of any amount up to ten dollars for the printing of souvenirs.' The following week the Merrymount Press turned out seventy-five copies of the first keepsake in this original series, ready for the talk on William Caslon by Walter Gilliss. With only a few breaks, the series continued until the first world war, as shown by the following checklist of items identified by catch-lines:

1] William Caslon portrait, meander of typographic flowers. 2 lvs., 4⅞ by 7½ inches. The Merrymount Press. 75 copies.

2] Standard trade terms used by photo-engravers. 4 lvs., 6½ by 4¼ inches. Arranged by C. F. Whitmarsh of *The Printing Art*. 75 copies.[64]

3] A keepsake in honour of Giambattista Bodoni, portrait. 2 lvs., 8⅜ by 5⅝ inches. 75 copies 'printed at the White Elephant, Hingham, the first impression from that establishment' by W. A. Dwiggins.

4] The Society will greet Mr. John Cotton Dana. Ich Dine decoration. 2 lvs., 9⅜ by 6¼ inches. H. L. Johnson.

5] The yarn of the Nancy Bell. 4lvs., 4½ by 3¼ inches. Sewn, in wrapper. Seaver-Howland Press. 75 copies.

6] A portrait of Horace Walpole. 2 lvs., tip-on, 9⅛ by 6¾ inches. D. B. Updike, at The Merrymount Press. 75 copies.

7] A page from Tagliente. 2 lvs., 8½ by 5¾ inches. The Heintzemann Press. 75 copies.

8] Color printing. 4 plates in printed envelope, 12½ by 9¾ inches. The Sparrell Print.

[64] This is the first piece of printing which makes provision for signatures of members attending the meeting. At the top of the sixth page appears the following: 'This Keepsake of the meeting of The Society of Printers, held at the City Club in Boston, Tuesday evening, March 4, 1913, belongs to Mr. [blank] and is passed on to his neighbor on the right for a voyage around the table, that on its return to his plate he may have documentary evidence of the fact that "among those present were the following:"' By means of this useful device we learn, from the Updike copy, that on his right was Henry L. Bullen, that there were twenty-three others present, and their identity.

The habit of collecting autographs antedated, and perhaps stimulated, inauguration of the keepsake series Updike brought back from the dinner meeting in New York on November 17, 1909, the special souvenir menu with twenty-one names written on it (see p. 55, also plate 5). Again, when the Society met at the Providence Art Club, November 22, 1911, the *Rhode-Island Almanack* that members carried away as a souvenir bore the names of fellow guests written on the back.

9] John Baskerville. 4 lvs. french fold, 9¼ by 6 inches. Addison C. Getchell & Son. 75 copies.

10] A portrait of Christophe Plantin. 2 lvs., 7½ by 5⅜ inches. The Athenæum Press. 75 copies.

11] A souvenir of Mr. Charles E. Goodspeed's talk. 9½ by 8 inches. Single leaf, tipped-on illustration. The Riverside Press. 75 copies.

12] Specimen des nouveau caracteres. 2 lvs., 9½ by 7 inches. The Christian Science Publishing Society. 75 copies.[65]

13] Printed on the occasion of a talk given by Mr. C. E. Lauriat, Jr. 2 lvs., 3¾ by 4½ inches.

14] The development of the woodcut. 2 lvs., 8¾ by 4¾ inches. The Heintzemann Press. 75 copies.[66]

15] Salve mcmxv. 4 lvs. french fold, 8½ by 5⅝ inches. Designed by Walt Harris, printed by A. C. Getchell & Son.

16] Society of Printers. 2 lvs., 8½ by 5¾ inches. Color halftone reproduction tipped on. McGrath-Sherrill Press. 75 copies.

17] A keepsake for the talk of Mr. Herbert L. Baker. 2 lvs., 4⅛ by 6 inches.

18] The first watermark. 4 lvs. french fold, 8½ by 5⅝ inches. The University Press. 75 copies.

19] Some leaves from an early chapter in the history of periodical publishing. 2 lvs., 7¾ by 4⅞ inches. Harvard University Press. 75 copies.

20] A keepsake for the visit . . . to the Widener Library. 2 lvs., 5½ by 7 inches.

21] [67] Printed on the occasion of a talk by Mr. Paul J.

[65] The reproduction of the title page and one other from the specimen book, 1819, of P. Didot, *l'aîné*, is accompanied by a printed slip with details concerning it.

[66] The illustration, signed P, has beneath it 'Courtesy of Alfred Bartlett.' Bartlett's 1914 catalogue advertises a design from a wood-block engraved by George Wolfe Plank. In recent years it turned up again in an advertisement in *Direct Advertising*.

[67] The souvenirs for the November 9, 1915, meeting included a copy of Ginn & Company's reprint of The New England Primer and of their booklet *Quality and Cost*. Since none is known to have been prepared

Sachs. 2 lvs., 8½ by 6 inches, with tip-on illustration. Harvard University Press. 75 copies.

22] Juno ad Romanos. 2 lvs., 11½ by 8¼ inches. 'Printed for the Society of Printers, Boston, Massachusetts. February 25, 1916' by John Cotton Dana (but see number 24 and note 68 below).

23] Reception and dinner to Mr. Timothy Cole. 2 lvs., 11⅝ by 8¼ inches, with tip-on illustration. The University Press. 75 copies.

24] This our noble art. 4 lvs. french fold, 8 by 6 inches. The University Press. 100 copies.[68]

25] Benjamin Sherbow. 4 lvs. french fold, 9½ by 6⅛ inches. Seaver-Howland Press. 75 copies.

26] Confessio Amantis. 4 lvs. french fold, 10⅛ by 7 inches. 'This Souvenir of the meeting of the Society of Printers, City Club, Boston, December 12, 1916, has been printed by hand for the members of the Society, by *Fred & Bertha Goudy*, at the *Village Press*, Forest Hills Gardens, Long Island, N. Y., from types designed by Mr. Goudy. 75 *copies*.'

27] Memento of a catalogue clinic. 2 lvs., 8⅞ by 6 inches, with drawing by H. Püterschein. The University Press. 75 copies.

28] Decorative design in typography. 4 lvs. french fold, 9¼ by 6⅛ inches. Designed by Walt Harris, printed by A. C. Getchell & Son.

29] The souvenir. 2 lvs., 9¼ by 7¼ inches, in the form of a miniature newspaper.

30] Souvenir of the visit . . . to Providence. 2 lvs., 6 by 4¾ inches, with tipped-on 'copy of the daguerreotype of Edgar Allan Poe taken in Providence . . . the day of his engagement. . . .'

especially for the Society, however, there is no entry in the keepsake series for this date. Similarly, the souvenirs for the May 23, 1916, meeting were etchings by George T. Plowman, speaker of the evening, provided by E. K. Robinson.

[68] A note on the back page contains this explanation: 'The address by Mr. Dana, planned for February 25, 1916 was postponed to April 7, 1916 and this souvenir distributed at that time.'

31] A souvenir of a talk 'Printing as a Factor in the War.' 2 lvs., 11¼ by 9½ inches (with the top folded down to make dimensions 8 by 9½). Seaver-Howland Press. 75 copies.

32] Some economic aspects of advertising. 4 lvs. french fold, 9½ by 6¼ inches. The Stetson Press.

33] For the Society of Printers and its guests. Photographic reproduction of the Massachusetts Institute of Technology main building façade, 14 by 11 inches, laid in folding printed cover. Prepared by Henry Lewis Johnson, M.I.T. '92. An omitted X makes the date 1907 instead of the correct year 1917.

34] Block printing and the graphic arts. 2 lvs., 9 by 5½ inches. Adapted from Mr. Preissig's designs by George F. Trenholm and printed by Addison C. Getchell & Son.

At this point the original series of keepsakes or souvenirs lapsed. The tendency to merge the advance notice of a meeting with a keepsake prepared for distribution in connection with it was irresistible. Wise old promoter that he was, Henry Lewis Johnson made sure of the December 18, 1917, meeting by getting out a four-page letterpress-printed announcement as well as the grand pictorial souvenir (number 33 in the preceding list). But more often the notice was mimeographed and sent out to members with a postcard on which they were expected to affix the two-cent wartime postage stamp for return to the secretary, with expression of their intention regarding the meeting.[69]

[69] For the great majority of meeting notices the typewriter or near-print duplicator was used. The exceptions signalize a quite special occasion to be announced or extraordinary zeal on the part of the man in charge. Thus, for example, Johnson saw to it that a neat printed notice was circulated for the Boston Public Library meeting in October 1923. Others of this period, properly printed, were for the New York–Jersey City pilgrimage in February 1926 and for talks by Thacher Nelson and Ashton Sanborn in November and December respectively of the ensuing season.

For the March 1919 meeting with the Boston Architectural Club, a handsome four-page circular was printed in black and red by the Merrymount Press. The same press prepared a similar announcement for the Joseph Pennell lecture the following February. Meanwhile a colorful notice of Arthur Allen's talk on the Munsell system, May 1919, was produced by the Berkeley Press; it was sent out in the form which was to prevail in later years, including name of speaker and topic, place and time of dinner (the euphemism 'social hour' had not appeared), and the secretary's exhortation to return the card so that he could make proper reservations.

With the national yearning for 'normalcy,' an effort to return to the limited edition souvenir was made following the election of E. K. Robinson as president in January 1923. For the first meeting under the new administration the Athenæum Press provided, in connection with George Parker Winship's talk on Caxton, a keepsake containing the old printer's blackletter advertisement decorated with the Red Pale sign, hand-rubricated. However, at the next month's meeting a combination was produced, demonstrating that the original souvenir series as instituted by Updike would not be revived. The piece featured a drawing by Walt Harris and was limited to a hundred copies in the good old-fashioned way but the letterpress inside welcomed Royal Bailey Farnum and said he 'will talk.' Although the lack of information as to the place and time was doubtless made up to the members by some other, and probably much more modest, notice, the confusion of purpose is evident. Anyway, those immediately concerned regarded it as a souvenir and showed appreciation for the artist and the printer, the Berkeley Press. As the secretary's minutes bear witness: 'The souvenir of this meeting was from a drawing by Walt Harris and it has attracted considerable attention both inside and outside of the Society.'

The 1927–1928 season started off with a notice of the talk by Winship on 'Morris to Morison,' printed by the new president, David T. Pottinger, at the Harvard University Press.[70] Further stirrings of ambition were reflected in a bright-hued poster fifteen inches long, designed by Dwiggins, heralding the December meeting on modernism in typography. There followed other souvenir-announcements, i.e., pieces which gave the essential information about the forthcoming meeting and at the same time exerted collector-appeal. The one for the January meeting was neatly printed by James G. Clarke, that for February by G. Gehman Taylor. For March there was a swashbuckling calligraphic announcement, and neat typography distinguished those for April and May. Thacher Nelson as secretary looked back with admiration on early examples and he commissioned work from competent members, offering terms much freer and easier than those governing the original series of keepsakes.[71]

But there are pitfalls to typographic as to other

[70] The reputation in America was still not great for the author of *Four Centuries*, published in 1924. That year Stanley Morison first visited America 'as a pilgrim, for the two volumes of *Printing Types* had been published in 1922.'

[71] In the final paragraph of a letter to Dwiggins dated November 23, 1927 Nelson wrote: 'I still treasure one of the few remaining copies of the notice which you made for the acrimonious debate which was more or less under the control of the late and very much lamented Mr. Seaver.' His reference is to the 'Memento of a Catalogue Clinic' described as number 27 in the original keepsake series list.

In the archives is Nelson's proposal to a fellow member that he print an announcement. Dated February 23, 1928, it reveals the going terms and conditions. 'Would you care to print the notices for the next meeting . . .' he inquires. 'We usually need only about 150 notices and are able to spend no more than $35 or $40 for printing. The stock, the type face, the number of colors, and the size, are left entirely to your judgment. . . .'

kinds of ambition. Early in the 1928–1929 season when Melbert B. Cary, Jr., came from New York to address the Society on 'Contemporary European Types and Printing,' the design and printing of the announcement fell to the lot of one of the most tradition-loving of members. He rose to the challenge with great resolution, to such effect as to draw anguished outcries: 'An analysis of any line, letter or word in the invitation shows it to violate every tradition of good type design and good taste,' a fellow member protested. 'I cannot believe that printing in general is to be degraded much longer or printers caused to waste good money for such types as used in this invitation.' Nelson suavely asked the complainant to design and print an early announcement, and the angry noises ceased in that quarter. However, when the printing bill came in there was more trouble, not so easy to dispose of; interestingly designed and produced pieces continued to appear throughout that season but then the president and treasurer tightened the purse strings. They recommended falling back on the cheap note-size announcement form.

The thirties opened with Thacher Nelson in the presidency. For a while the announcements were reminiscent in certain respects of the old keepsakes he liked. They had individuality. For the first meeting, October 1930, the number was limited to seventy copies. A hundred were printed for the November meeting. But Depression-style near-print soon regained the ascendancy and except for special events, such as the thirtieth annual meeting, in June 1935, featuring the Merrymount Press exhibition at the Boston Public Library, the printing press in the service of the Society took a long sabbatical. This was no fault of Daniel B. Bianchi who, on becoming secretary in 1933, had begun to press for at least an occasional properly printed notice. Three years later the proposal received sympathetic attention when G. Gehman Taylor was installed as president. Taylor himself launched the revival by contributing the notice for the December 1936 meeting.

From that time forward the announcement-keepsakes have generally been levied upon members rather than commissioned from them. In the words since become familiar in presidential reports, these productions are contributed 'without expense to the Society' — drawings, plates, paper, and printing, usually by several donors. So instituted and accepted as a sort of tax, they have appeared with relatively few lapses in connection with meetings through the succeeding score of vicissitudinous years.

Interesting sidelights on the history of the Society's meeting notices and souvenirs are offered by a letter from Henry Lewis Johnson to the secretary. He wrote on October 20, 1937, from Acworth, New Hampshire, where he died a few weeks later.

'The fine notice of the Goudy meeting has been forwarded to me. I am sorry that I will be unable to attend.

'I have known Mr. Goudy since the beginning of his notable career in the graphic arts. Please give him my affectionate regards and my regrets at not being able to see him on this occasion. . . .

'It is probable that I will make one or two trips to Boston or New York during the coming months and I will count on meeting up with members of the Society of Printers — and to attend meetings whenever our dates coincide.

'Please send a copy of Mr. Goudy's souvenir to me. I have a considerable file of notices of meetings which I will put in order and send to the Society for its records.'

It is to be observed that Johnson clearly distinguishes between the notice for this meeting, which was a rubricated leaflet dressed in Goudy types and ornaments, and the souvenir of the meeting which he evidently expected Goudy to bring for presentation at the gathering. The file of notices he intended to give to the Society for its records was unfortunately not delivered and has not been located.

Half a century of printers' printing, done for their Society dedicated to the advancement of printing as an art, ought to present an instructive and significant exhibition. Here the printer, within obvious limits, could find freedom beyond the routine confinements if he chose to look for it. He could, on such an occasion, give all to craftsmanship and let front-office prudence go hang. His inspiration for the design of a four-page keepsake might fly away with him to exhilarating and possibly dizzy heights. His work, this once anyway, whether plain or fancy, skilled or awkward, low-brow or rarefied aesthetic, ought to stand for him and reflect his attitude toward printing.

Whatever a member or combination of members turned out would of course come under critical scrutiny by the group. A sampling in these pages again (and less fairly in reproduction on paper and in inks other than their own) brings specimens to pass in review. Most of the current commentary, being unrecorded (and occasionally unprintable), in response to these modest pieces in the souvenir-announcement sequence, is lost to history, though there are documents preserved on the introduction of the New Typography in the twenties, as mentioned a page or so earlier.[72] It is perfectly apparent, however, that

[72] See page 92. Part of J. Horace McFarland's letter of November 9, 1928, deserves to be quoted in this connection:
'The invitation is, I know, in the "modern manner" which substi-

hospitality was shown to innovation, that the stranger was taken in and given a hearing — a courtesy not always reciprocated by the sharp-elbowed modernist crowd, whose apostles were in sooth sometimes pretty strange. The Boston-centered group has always done its share of independent typographic thinking and has consequently not been generally overmuch impressed by the last word of imported fashion.[73]

tutes noise for music, the vagaries of an ill-taught draftsman for art, obscure slop for literature, and does other violences to that enduring good taste upon which, after all, we do depend, and to which we eventually return.

'But I had not expected the Society of Printers to submit to such a tendency, for which no claims can be made save that it is noisy and "modern". . . .'

Replied the secretary, Thacher Nelson:

'I agree with you, personally, in all that you say about modern art, although I must confess that I entertain a youthful and doubtless sinful enthusiasm for jazz as dance music.

'Mr. Sherrill, who printed the invitation is, like myself, constitutionally an Englishman of the eighteenth century.

'However, we believe that Mr. Cary is coming to talk to us about the kind of thing which is represented by the invitation which warns you of his approach. That kind of thing exists, and must be considered, discussed, evaluated, and pored over for whatever of value it may contain. . . .

'You will probably tell me that I am a Jesuit and that I am attempting to justify the means by the end, and while this may be true, the means are, after all, not so terrible that they are going to cause any actual suffering except to you and me, while they have the great value of bringing out such frank opinions as that expressed in your letter.

'. . . In order that your own views may have adequate expression, would you be willing to produce an invitation for one of the forthcoming meetings . . .?'

[73] The clever young American designer Paul Rand, writing recently in the British *Penrose Annual* (London, 1949) on 'Modern and Traditional Typography in America,' states the view of advanced New Yorkers: 'One cannot deprecate the contributions made by such men as Goudy, Rogers, Dwiggins, Cleland, etc.,' he allows magnanimously. 'To say, however, that any of these men is creative in the vernacular of the twentieth century is certainly an error in classification.' If Dwiggins could be induced to turn his attention back to advertising design there is little doubt of his ability, as proved by past performance, to beat the youngsters at their own game single-handed — to say nothing of book design, and of the other veterans riskily challenged. Updike was also often attacked by the self-styled modernists (who

The meeting notice and the hybrid keepsake-announcement, to return to cases, are indisputably in the publicity category and distinctly different in purpose from the souvenir or keepsake simple. Although publicity, they are addressed to a rather special public; moreover, whether properly or not, some of them carry an air of expecting to pass the wastebasket test, that is, to mount at least the first rung on the way to acceptance as works of art. This hybrid form — it deserves a harsher name high among the B's — should it put across the message with a two-fisted typographic jolt? Should it flatter and charm its recipient as one belonging to a select group? The exhibition suggests the increasing reliance on knock-'em-stiff-and-drag-'em-in as compared with the less strident and often more imaginative production.

Anyhow, when the right designer and printer get together (ideally in the same individual) the result may turn out to be treasurable whatever its category. The fact is perfectly demonstrated in the menu for the dinner given to Rudolph Ruzicka on January 16, 1951. This all-Ruzicka graphic confection is a rich and tasteful souvenir of the occasion, as full of Ruzicka's style as the brief words in which he responded to the Society's salute.

In sum, taking all together the printing of every kind done in the name of the Society of Printers throughout its first half century, the standards of

averred that the ornamental leaf appearing on his title pages was to cover a nudity of typographic inventiveness), but never to his face for danger of a mordant wit and shrewd tongue. One time when he was sitting at his desk talking to a visitor the telephone rang; he broke off and lifted the receiver. 'Yes' he said, as an expression of mock consternation spread over his features, 'What happened? my God, man! what happened?' Smartly he hung up and swung round in his chair. 'It was —' (he named the scholarly head of a renowned press) 'asking whether I'd found this Society of Printers notice in the morning's mail. He said he was just trying something modern!'

design, materials, and workmanship are incontestably superior to the general level. Insofar as this claim can fairly be carried, the Society offers tangible proof of the values in its program, which is centrally the self-improvement of members in their chosen field through studying and working together for the advancement of printing as an art. By such a yardstick the measure of 'the most distinguished association of printers in America' (as Bullen wrote of it) may be taken with confidence on its fiftieth birthday.

Appendix and Index

Calendar of Meetings

1905

February 14 Hotel Victoria. Organization, adoption of constitution, election of council.

March 13 University Club, dinner.

May 8 Boston Athletic Association. Otto Fleischner, on the proposed publication of a bibliography of printing.

1906

January 26 On Italian printers.

March 22 4 Joy Street. On technical education.

April 27 Denman W. Ross.

December 18 City Club.

1907

January 25 A. D. Little, on paper.

December 2 Chickering Hall. T. J. Cobden-Sanderson, 'The Book Beautiful.'

1908

November 10 Annual meeting.

December 7 Discussion of the Pamphlet.

1909

February 1 Exhibition of line plate illustration.

March 1 H. L. Koopman, on book papers.

April 5 Walter Sargent, on examples of design and printing in public schools.

May 11 Providence visit. A. W. Pollard.

June 1 H. T. Bailey, report on the Pamphlet.

November 16 & 17 New York visit. Dinner at the Players Club.

December 14 Cambridge. Dinner at Harvard Union. Treasure Room, University Library.

1910

January 4 Discussion of the need for a university course in printing.

March 29 Discussion of preceding topic.

November 10 H. T. Bailey, 'Harmony of Color.'
December 13 Cambridge, new building of the Harvard Lampoon and University Library. Dinner at the Harvard Union. W. C. Lane on his course on the history of the printed book.

1911

January 7 Frank French, on American wood-engraving.
March 8 Annual meeting. Modern German printing.
October 31 Discussion of the Pamphlet, also of the possible Harvard course.
November 14 Annual meeting. J. W. Baird, on legibility of letters.
November 22 Providence. Book collection at Providence Public Library. Dinner at Providence Art Club.

1912

January 25 D. B. Updike, on early industrial conditions and their effect on typography.
February 6 W. C. Huebner, on offset printing.
February 13 H. L. Bullen, on the roman alphabet and its use in design.
March 2 J. H. McFarland, guest; discussion of how to make the Harvard course known.
May 7 C. S. Olcott, on getting photographic illustrations for a special edition of Scott.
November 7 Annual meeting. Books printed by Charles Whittingham.
December 7 Salem visit. Dinner at the Salem Club. Ross Turner, on the illumination of books.
December 28 Print department, Boston Museum of Fine Arts.

1913

January 29 C. L. Nichols, on Isaiah Thomas.
February 11 Walter Gilliss, on Caslon's life and work.
March 4 H. L. Bullen, 'Specimen Books of the Early Typefounders.'
April 22 T. M. Cleland, 'The Italian Printer Bodoni.'
May 20 J. C. Dana, 'Modern Revival of Printing in Germany.'
October 23 Robert Seaver, on chapbooks.
November 14 Annual meeting. Lewis Buddy, III, on Horace Walpole.

December 29 New clubhouse of Harvard Club of Boston. W. A. Dwiggins, on early writing books and modern calligraphy.

1914

January 30 A. W. Elson, on color printing.
February 24 Boston Art Club. J. H. Benton, on John Baskerville.
March 25 H. L. Koopman, on the Plantin Museum.
April 28 C. E. Goodspeed, 'American Pictorial Illustration 1775–1875.'
May 28 T. M. Cleland, on the work of the Didots.
October 15 C. E. Lauriat, 'International Exhibition in Leipsic.'
November 10 Annual meeting. W. M. Ivins, Jr., on the woodcut 1490–1540.

1915

January 7 The Boston City Club. C. H. Walker, 'Historic Ornament in Its Relation to Printing.'
February 18 The Boston City Club. W. H. Bowker, on the making of three-color halftones.
March 4 H. L. Baker, 'Recent Developments in the Manufacture and Operation of Printing Presses.'
April 9 S. A. Kimber, 'Significance of Paper Watermarks in the Middle Ages.'
May 11 Donald Scott, 'Publishing.'
May 19 The Boston City Club. Special meeting to discuss New York trip.
May 24 & 25 New York visit. Hotel Vanderbilt. Dinner by the American Institute of Graphic Arts.
October 14 Cambridge, Widener Library. Dinner at the Colonial Club.
November 9 Annual meeting, Cambridge Y.M.C.A. E. K. Robinson, 'Schoolbooks.'
December 2 Colonial Club, Cambridge. Fogg Art Museum. P. J. Sachs, 'Early Italian Engraving.'

1916

January 11 Boston Art Club. E. R. Currier, 'Laying Out Job Composition.' Remarks by F. W. Goudy.
March 21 Colonial Club, Cambridge. Fogg Art Museum. Timothy Cole, 'The Analogy Between Wood Engraving and Painting.'
April 7 The Boston City Club. J. C. Dana, 'Librarians as Printers.'

May 23 Boston Art Club. George T. Plowman, 'Etching.'

October 10 The Boston City Club. (Intended farewell for Bruce Rogers but he was detained by illness.)

November 14 The Boston City Club. Benjamin Sherbow, 'Type-use in Advertising.'

December 12 The Boston City Club. F. W. Goudy, 'Type Design.'

1917

January 16 Hotel Avery. T. F. Fennessy, on aspects of the paper situation, and C. A. Gorman, 'Inks.'

February 20 The Boston City Club. 'Catalogue Clinic.'

March Goodspeed's on Park Street. Walter Dorwin Teague, 'Design in Typography.'

April 17 The Boston City Club. Edward McKernon, 'How to Read a Newspaper.'

May 16 Providence trip. Dinner at the University Club.

October 10 The Boston Athenæum. C. K. Bolton, 'Printing as a Factor in the War.' Dinner at the City Club.

November 13 The Boston City Club. Perry Walton, 'Some Economic Aspects of Advertising.'

December 18 Central Building, M.I.T. John Ritchie, Jr., description of buildings and departments.

1918

January 22 The Boston City Club. FitzRoy Carrington, 'Work of Claude Mellan and Jean Morin.'

February 19 The Boston City Club. W. A. Dwiggins, 'How Would You Lay Out This Job.'

March 29 The Boston Architectural Club. F. C. Brown, 'When to Use Lettering.'

May 2 The Boston City Club. J. B. Scott, 'What the Printer Should Do to Get Better Results from Electrotypes.'

June 3 Colonial Club. C. C. Lane, 'History and Development of the Harvard Press'; Arthur Pope, 'Theory of Color with Reference to the Printer's Problem.'

November 19 Annual meeting, The Boston City Club. Vojtěch Preissig, 'Block Printing and the Use of Linoleum for Engraving Poster Work.'

December 30 Informal discussion of current specimens of printed matter.

1919

January 14 The Boston City Club. Ford Hall. Discussion of dyestuffs for ink-making (with Craftsmen Club and Typothetæ).

February 18 Boston Museum of Fine Arts. Loring Dunn, on contents of Museum and opportunities it could offer to printers.

March 27 The Boston Architectural Club. Joint meeting with Architectural Club. Discussion of War Memorials.

May 8 Walker Memorial, Little Laboratory, M.I.T. H. J. Skinner, 'Paper-Making.'

May 27 The Boston Architectural Club. Joint meeting with Society of Architects. Arthur S. Allen, 'Relation of the Munsell System of Color to Printing and Advertising.'

October 27 Annual meeting, The Boston City Club. Guest, J. F. DeChant.

December 22 Boston Shoe Trades Club. Discussion of possible children's typography textbook.

1920

January 23 Boston Art Club. Farewell dinner to W. M. Stone.

February 20 Unity House. Joseph Pennell, 'American Illustration in the Past, in the Present — and Will There Be Any in the Future?'

April 22 Providence visit. University Club. H. L. Koopman, 'Books Useful to a Printer.'

November 12 Rogers Building, 491 Boylston Street. H. L. Johnson, G. P. Winship.

1921

February 14 Rogers Building. F. Chase, 'Books for Printers in the Boston Public Library.'

December 28 Signet Society, Cambridge. E. Byrne Hackett, 'How It Seems To Be a Bookseller; and How the Court of Last Resort, the Customer, Reacts to Fine Printing and Well-made Books.'

1922

January 20 Boston Art Club. W. A. Dwiggins, 'Ornament.'

March 29 Boston Art Club. H. L. Bullen, 'Aldus Manutius.'

May 16 Boston Art Club. G. P. Winship, 'Estienne Family.'

1923

January 30 Boston Art Club. L. C. Gandy, 'Simplicity in Typography.'

March 8 Boston Art Club. G. P. Winship, 'Caxton.'

May 17 Boston Art Club. R. B. Farnum, 'Art in Printing, from the Layman's Point of View.'

October 2 Boston Public Library. Walter Rowlands, on works on printing in the Library; C. F. D. Belden, on books and printing; H. L. Johnson and D. B. Updike on books printed by Updike in the collection. Dinner at Boston Art Club.

November 20 Hall of the Harvard Lampoon Building. W. B. Wheelwright, account of the building.

1924

January 14 Boston Art Club. E. W. Greene, 'Engraving and Printing Departments of Wentworth Institute.'

February 7 Dinner at Boston Art Club. Lecture by C. P. Rollins at the Normal Art School. (One of a series of nine lectures. See p. 62.)

April 24 Boston Art Club. R. T. Hale, on recent trip to England and the Continent, printing and publishing.

May 1 Annual meeting, 95 St. James Avenue. Plans for commercial printing exhibit.

May 19 95 St. James Avenue. W. M. Gordon, Contemporary Commercial Printing Exhibit.

May 21 Providence. Spring pilgrimage.

1925

January 6 Harvard Club. Home of Davenport Brown, 196 Beacon Street. G. P. Winship, on printers represented in the collection.

February 10 Dinner at Harvard Union, Cambridge. Widener Library. G. P. Winship, 'European and American Contemporary Books.'

March 10 95 St. James Avenue. Boston Public Library. H. L. Johnson, on merits of Fifty Best Books of 1924.

April 7 Boston Art Club. W. A. Dwiggins, on early days of the Society, and H. L. Bullen, on experiences abroad and collected treasures.

May 7 Olde Grey House, Anderson Street. L. C. Gandy, on printing by J. H. Nash.

October 28 Harvard Club.

December 15 Boston Art Club. E. K. Robinson, on European books. H. L. Bullen, on books in the library of American Typefounders Company.

1926

February 10 & 11 New York trip.

March 2 The Boston City Club. H. T. Bailey.

April 3 Exhibition room, Boston Chamber of Commerce. H. L. Bullen, 'Recent European Printing.'

May 18 Annual meeting, Rogers Building. W. Emerson's book, 'Roman Bridges.'

September 27 Dinner at the Boston Art Club. Boston Public Library. Henry Guppy, 'Stepping Stones to the Art of Typography.'

November 9 University Club, 40 Trinity Place. Thacher Nelson, 'Some of the Influence of Copperplate Engraving on Modern Printing Types.'

December 8 Ashton Sanborn, 'How Can the Museum of Fine Arts Serve the Printers of Boston?'

1927

January 11 University Club. Duncan Phillips, 'The History of the Riverside Press.'

February 16 Dinner at the Boston City Club. Goodspeed's, Ashburton Place. C. E. Goodspeed, on collecting.

March 17 University Club. C. P. Rollins, 'What Next in Printing.'

April 7 Dinner at the University Club. Boston Public Library. D. T. Pottinger, on the Fifty Books of the Year.

April 28 Boston Art Club.

May 31 Annual meeting, Boston Art Club. Maurice A. Blackmur, on 'The Possibilities of Modern Printing Papers.'

October 20 Signet Society, Cambridge. G. P. Winship, 'From Morris to Morison.'

December 9 University Club. H. L. Gage, 'Modernism in Typography.'

1928

January 10 Boston Art Club. Private library evening.

February 9 The Boston City Club. F. G. Melcher, on adventures in taste.

March 27 Signet Society, Cambridge. Symposium on calligraphy.

April 28 Salem visit. Dinner at Hotel Hawthorne.

May 21 Annual meeting, University Club. Frederic Warde, on European printing houses.

October 1 Luncheon meeting. Durgin & Park, Hayward Place. Jordan Marsh Co., for Fifty Books of 1928.

October 10 Dinner at Boston Chamber of Commerce. Private view of A. I. G. A. exhibition of Commercial Printing.

November 13 Boston Art Club. M. B. Cary, Jr., on contemporary European types and printing.

December 28 Holiday Dinner. Otto's Broad Street Inn. *Divertissement* by the President.

1929

January 29 Boston Art Club. Museum of Fine Arts. Ashton Sanborn.

March 8 University Club. Meeting in honor of D. B. Updike.

April 25 Providence Pilgrimage. Dinner at the Faculty Club.

May 28 Annual meeting. Boston Art Club. G. P. Winship, 'The Fifty Books of 1928.'

October 23 University Club. M. B. Cary, Jr., on current European typographic trends.

November 21 Boston Art Club. A. F. Mackay, on some of the larger European printing plants.

1930

January 27 University Club. Paul Hollister, 'Current Tendencies in the Graphic Arts.'

March 28 Worcester Pilgrimage. Dinner at Hotel Bancroft. L. C. Wroth, on colonial printing.

April 30 Boston Art Club. John Simon.

May 15 Annual meeting. Dinner at University Club. Exhibit in new Treasure Room, Boston Public Library.

September 29 Meeting with Typothetæ to meet George W. Jones.

October 2 Chamber of Commerce. T. J. Helleberg, demonstration of hand binding.

October 15 University Club. L. B. Siegfried.

November 20 Dinner at Boston City Club. L. A. Holman, at his print shop, Park Street.

1931

January 8 Dinner at the Harvard Union, Cambridge. Private library meeting at the Signet Society.

March 26 George Marsh, on illustration.

May 26 Annual meeting, University Club. Boston Public Library for Fifty Books exhibition.

October 29 Sidney C. Woodward, on prints.

November 24 University Club. D. T. Pottinger, 'Printing and Publishing in Boston 1880–1930.'

December 4 University Club. C. P. Rollins, 'Historic Printing Offices.'

1932

January 5 University Club. Films, 'Last of the Wood-engravers' and 'The Etcher's Art.'

March 11 Hilary D. C. Pepler.

April 12 J. M. Hunnewell's private library, 14 Chestnut Street. Buffet supper at home of W. B. Wheelwright, 5 Strong Place.

May 10 Dinner at Boston Art Club. Home of Mrs. A. P. Loring, 2 Gloucester Street. Marbled papers.

June 7 Annual meeting. Dinner at the University Club. Public Library, Fifty Books exhibit.

October 27 Massachusetts Horticultural Society Library.

November 29 Society of Arts and Crafts galleries, 9 Park Street.

December 20 Fogg Art Museum print room. Miss Laura Dudley.

1933

February 3 Milton Academy Library.

February 17 E. P. Goldschmidt.

November 23 Boston Public Library. Exhibit of French eighteenth-century engravings and books.

December 14 Rockwell Kent, 'Why This Modern?'

1934

January 26 Joint meeting with Boston Club of Printing House Craftsmen, Tileston & Hollingsworth calendar.

April 10 W. D. Teague, auspices Boston Advertising Club.

May 7 Boston College Library, Chestnut Hill. Rev. W. M. Stinson, stained glass, books.

October 10 Annual meeting. American Unitarian Association, 25 Beacon Street. W. Forbes Robertson.

November 27 Bostonian Society, Old State House. G. R. Marvin, on Bostonian Society's collection.

December 5 University Club. Boston Public Library exhibit of Cambridge University Press printing.

December 10 Boston Public Library. Private viewing of Four Centuries exhibit.

1935

January 24 Holman's Print Shop. Louis Holman, on the history of print making.

June 12 Dinner at the Boston Art Club. Boston Public Library, review of year's activities.

October 23 Lincoln, Gallery of Julian de Cordova. Exhibit of art objects.

1936

January 3 Christian Science Publishing Society. H. A. Morton, 'History of the Bible.'

February 11 Capitoline Restaurant, 10 Derne Street. Thacher Nelson, 'History of Type Design.'

February 29 Gardner Museum. Morris Carter, showing of the collection.

March 26 University Club. C. P. Rollins, 'Whither Now, Typographer?'

April 16 The Boston City Club. L. B. Siegfried, 'The Story of the Present Format of *The American Printer* and a Comment on Current Typography.'

June 18 Boston Art Club. Alec Miller, 'A Sculptor's View of History.'

October 15 Boston Art Club. Hans Mardersteig, on the Officina Bodoni.

November 17 University Club. W. C. Doebbelin, demonstration of the making of marble papers.

December 17 Boston Art Club. P. A. Bennett, 'Making of Fine Books.'

1937

January 12 Boston Art Club. H. C. Merrill, 'Old Time Wood-engravers and Their Work.'

February 18 University Club. Lucian Bernhard, 'Why New Type Faces?'

March 18 University Club. F. C. Sherman, 'From Gutenberg to Rogers.'

April 22 University Club. Warren Chappell, 'The Nice Printer in a Modern World.'

May 20 Annual meeting. Boston Art Club. Informal discussion of books and prints.

October 21 The Boston City Club. F. W. Goudy, 'Types and Type Design.'

November 18 The Boston City Club. W. D. Orcutt, 'Celebrities Off Parade.'

1938

January 25 University Club. W. M. Gordon, 'An Informal Talk on Bill Dwiggins.'

February 25 The Boston City Club. Gerry Powell, 'Which Way Typography?'

April 4 The Boston City Club. P. A. Bennett, 'The Fifty Books.'

April 21 Schrafft's, 16 West Street. Milton Glick, 'A 20th Century Style in Book Design?'

May 10 Annual meeting. Boston Art Club. Hobby night for members.

October 21 Schrafft's. H. N. King, on typography.

November 29 Schrafft's. Valenti Angelo.

1939

January 19 Signet Society, Cambridge. Philip Hofer, on Rudolph Ruzicka.

February 23 Schrafft's. Walter Gropius, 'Creative Design.'

March 23 Schrafft's. P. A. Bennett, 'The Fifty Books.'

May 25 Annual meeting. Schrafft's. Members' night.

October 19 M.I.T. Graduate House. Dard Hunter, on making paper by hand.

November 13 Providence visit. Brown University. Exhibit, The Art and Craft of Printing. C. P. Rollins, speaker.

November 17 Schrafft's. Helen Gentry, exhibit of her work.

1940

January 18 Signet Society. Philip Hofer, on the new Department of Printing and Graphic Arts at Harvard.

February 16 Schrafft's. Edmund Thompson, 'Functions of the Small Press.'

March 15 Schrafft's. P. A. Bennett, 'The Fifty Books.'

April 18 Schrafft's. Warren Chappell, 'A Viewpoint on Type and Illustration.'

May 24 University Club. Exhibit of Updike's work at the Boston Public Library.

October 24 Schrafft's. D. T. Pottinger, 'Five Hundred Years of Printing.'

November 14 Schrafft's. John Begg, 'You Can't Judge a Book by Its Cover.'

1941

January 23 Schrafft's. T. M. Cleland.

March 4 Fogg Museum. Exhibit of Chinese and Japanese prints.

March 27 Signet Society. P. A. Bennett, 'The Fifty Books.'

April 24 Schrafft's. E. S. Lipsett, 'Modern Trends of Printing and Advertising Techniques.'

May 22 Annual meeting. Schrafft's. A. J. Bailey, showing of film.

October 8 University Club. A. W. Heintzelman, 'The Wiggin Collection of Prints.'

November 13 Schrafft's. E. Trotter, 'Printing under Wartime Conditions.'

1942

January 22 Schrafft's. Ray Nash, 'Liberal Education and the Printer.'

February 13 Schrafft's. W. D. Orcutt, testimonial dinner.

March 26 Schrafft's. P. A. Bennett, 'The Fifty Books.'

April 23 Schrafft's. Auction sale of books.

May 5 Dinner at the Harvard Faculty Club. Houghton Library, ladies' night.

May 28 Schrafft's. Beatrice Warde.

October 15 Schrafft's. D. T. Pottinger, 'What Next in Printing?'

November 19 Schrafft's. Paul Standard, 'Calligraphy.'

1943

January 21 Schrafft's. W. E. Rudge, Jr., on *Print*.

March 25 Schrafft's. P. A. Bennett, 'The Fifty Books.'

April 15 Schrafft's. C. E. Sherman, 'Is Fine Printing a Sacred Cow?'

May 20 Annual meeting. Schrafft's.

October 13 Schrafft's. G. H. Edgell, 'Certain Masterpieces in the Museum of Fine Arts.'

November 10 Schrafft's. Evelyn Harter Glick, 'Printers as Men of the World.'

1944

February 9 Schrafft's. Melvin Loos, 'Observations of the Printing Profession.'

March 8 Schrafft's. Hugo Steiner-Prag, on his own work with books.

April 12 Schrafft's. Arthur Thompson, 'The Fifty Books.'

May 11 Annual meeting. G. P. Winship, 'The Past and Future of the Society of Printers.'

October 11 Engineers Club, 2 Commonwealth Avenue. J. H. Benson, 'The Letters We Use.'

November 8 Engineers Club. Karl Kup, 'The Spencer Collection in the New York Public Library.'

1945

February 14 Engineers Club. Ernst Reichl, 'Comments on Typography in Books and Advertising.'

March 14 Harvard Club. A. P. Tedesco, 'The Renaissance of Book Illustration in America.'

April 11 Engineers Club. Arthur Thompson, 'The Fifty Books.'

May 9 Hotel Lenox. Fortieth Anniversary meeting. Past presidents' night.

October 3 Engineers Club. Fritz Eichenberg.

November 7 Engineers Club. H. Z. Walck, 'Publishing in the British War Zone.'

1946

January 7 Fox & Hounds Club, 448 Beacon Street. F. G. Melcher.

February 6 Engineers Club. C. H. Griffith, 'Postwar Type Matters.'

March 6 Engineers Club. Joseph P. Donovan, 'Modern Photo-Engraving.'

April 3 Engineers Club. P. A. Bennett, 'The Fifty Books.'

May 1 Annual meeting. Engineers Club. Roger Mame.

November 6 Engineers Club. Paul McPharlin, 'Is Advertising Printing Design Abreast of the Times?'

December 4 Engineers Club. E. D. Chase, 'A Christmas Tradition.'

1947

January 13 Printing and Publishing Week. Joint meeting with the Boston Bookbuilders, Boston Club of Printing House Craftsmen, and the Graphic Arts Institute of Massachusetts.

February 5 Engineers Club. Brad Stephens, 'Town Reports.'

March 5 Engineers Club. George Marsh, 'New Methods and Materials and their Influence on Style.'

April 2 Engineers Club. Watson Gordon, 'Fine Printing on a Commercial Basis.'

May 7 Engineers Club. B. L. Stratton, on 'The Fifty Books.'

October 22 Engineers Club. Arthur F. Williams, on some of the books he has designed.

November 14 Hampshire House, 84 Beacon Street. Reginald Orcutt, 'Our Fellow-Craftsmen Overseas.'

1948

April 7 Engineers Club. J. Ellery French, 'Precision Plastic Plates.'

May 5 Engineers Club. W. D. McKenzie and Mrs. McKenzie, 'Art Reproductions by Silk Screen.'

October 6 Engineers Club. Kurt H. Volk, on advertising typography.

November 10 Parker House. Arnold Bank, 'Calligraphy, Lettering and Type.'

December 1 Engineers Club. Arthur Thompson, 'The Textbooks of the Year.'

1949

February 2 Dard Hunter Paper Museum, Massachusetts Institute of Technology.

March 14 Signet Society. James Wardrop, 'The Italian Writing Masters of the XVIth Century.'

April 5 Engineers Club. Joint meeting with the Boston Bookbuilders. H. L. Gage on 'The Fifty Books.'

April 19 Trip to the Rumford Press, Concord, New Hampshire.

May 4 Annual meeting. Engineers Club. Film showing.

October 5 Ninety-nine Club, 99 State Street. Membership participation night.

November 2 Ninety-nine Club. Oscar Ogg, 'Lettering in Bookwork.'

December 7 Ninety-nine Club. Discussion of newer things in the craft.

1950

January 17 Town House, 100 Warrenton Street. Rollins exhibition.

February 1 Ninety-nine Club. R. Josephy, 'The Traveling Designer'; and Paul Barter, 'Printing Experiences Overseas During World War II.'

March 1 Ninety-nine Club. Milton Zudek, on the use of type in advertising.

April 5 Boston Public Library Treasure Room. H. L. Gage, on 'The Fifty Books.'

May 3 Annual meeting. Ninety-nine Club. Movie night.

October 1 Ninety-nine Club. C. Matlack Price, 'The Art Student and the Graphic Arts.'

November 1 Ninety-nine Club. Members' night, 'Brickbats and Bouquets.'

December 6 Ninety-nine Club. 'Bookbinders' Rodeo,' panel discussion.

1951

January 16 Joseph's Restaurant, 279 Dartmouth Street. Dinner in honor of Rudolph Ruzicka. Exhibit at Boston Public Library.

February 7 Ninety-nine Club. Daniel Melcher, 'How to Sell Me (and Other Buyers) More Printing.'

March 7 Ninety-nine Club. William Guth and E. H. Hugo, 'Sidelights on Contone and Collotype.'

April 4 Joseph's Restaurant. Bror Zachrisson, on 'The Fifty Books.'

May 9 Annual meeting. Ninety-nine Club. "Vic" Johnson, 'Sport Cartoon Highlights.'

October 3 Dinner at the Country Fare, Hingham. Visit to Dwiggins' studio.

November 7 Dinner at Hartwell Farms, Lincoln. Visit to the De Cordova & Dana Museum. F. P. Walkey, 'Changing Concepts in Design.'

December 5 Ninety-nine Club. F. W. Young and W. F. Johnston, film 'Fine Binding.' Hannah D. French, 'Binding of the Past.'

1952

January 14 School of the Museum of Fine Arts. Russell Smith, 'Basic Design.' Dorothy Abbe, on the Commercial Printing course.

February 6 Ninety-nine Club. Marshall Lee, 'Design, Typography and Smoke.'

March 5 Supper at the Club of Odd Volumes. Boston Athenæum, Veronica Ruzicka show. W. M. Whitehill, on the Library.

April 17 & 18 New York trip. Visits at the New York Public Library, Spencer collection; Morgan Library; Columbia University; and the Grolier Club.

April 23 Hotel Lenox. F. G. Melcher, on 'The Fifty Books.'

May 7 Dinner at the Oakley Country Club, Watertown. Visit to the Library of the late Chester Noyes Greenough, Belmont.

May 21 Annual meeting. Ninety-nine Club. Ellsworth Geist, 'Why Do We Need Design?'

October 1 Hotel Vendome. Dorothy Abbe, on some of the books of 1952.

November 15 Providence visit. Visits at the Providence Public Library; John Carter Brown Library; and the Annmary Brown Memorial Library.

November 22 Dartmouth College trip. G. W. Ovink, 'After All, What Does Functional Typography Mean?'

December 3 Dinner at the Harvard Faculty Club. Houghton Library. Philip Hofer, on exhibits in the library.

1953

February 4 Hotel Vendome. W. J. Stevens, 'The Merits of Offset Lithography.'

March 18 Dinner at the Hotel Vendome. Institute of Contemporary Art. C. F. Zahn, 'Integrated Design Programs in Industry.'

April 29 Hotel Lenox. Ronald W. Murray, on 'The Fifty Books.'

May 21 Annual meeting. Ninety-nine Club. Beatrice Warde, 'The Future of Typography and How You Can Affect It.'

September 23 Hotel Vendome. Jackson Burke, 'Printing Uninhibited' exhibit.

October 28 Ninety-nine Club. Stanley Rice, 'Textbook Design.'

December 1 Dinner at the Hotel Kenmore. Simmons College. James Wardrop, 'The Script of Humanism.'

1954

February 3 Ninety-nine Club. Howard King, on the Intertype Fotosetter.

March 10 Ninety-nine Club. Hellmut Lehmann-Haupt, on the Constance Missal.

April 7 Hotel Vendome. Alvin Eisenman, on 'The Fifty Books.'

May 5 Annual meeting. Harvard Club of Boston. Discussion of members' work.

October 6 Ninety-nine Club. Albert Kner, 'Package Design.'

November 3 Dinner at Pillar House, Newton Lower Falls. Visit to the Wellesley College Library, for a special showing of books by Bruce Rogers and books from the Grabhorn Press, as guests of Hannah D. French.

December 1 Ninety-nine Club. O. Alfred Dickman, 'Newspaper Production.'

List of Officers

1905–1906
WILLIAM DANA ORCUTT, *President*
BRUCE ROGERS, *Vice-President*
HENRY LEWIS JOHNSON, *Secretary*
* FREDERICK D. NICHOLS, *Treasurer*

1906–1907
(Records incomplete)

1907–1908
(Records incomplete)

1908–1910
HENRY LEWIS JOHNSON, *President*
W. H. GREELEY, *Vice-President*
C. C. LANE, *Secretary*
J. ALBERT BRIGGS, *Treasurer*

1910–1911
HENRY LEWIS JOHNSON, *President*
W. H. GREELEY, *Vice-President*
C. C. LANE, *Secretary*
J. ALBERT BRIGGS, *Treasurer*

1911–1912
HENRY LEWIS JOHNSON, *President*
GEORGE P. TILTON, *Vice-President*
C. C. LANE, *Secretary*
J. ALBERT BRIGGS, *Treasurer*

1912–1913
DANIEL BERKELEY UPDIKE, *President*
HENRY LEWIS JOHNSON, *Vice-President*
C. C. LANE, *Secretary*
ROBERT SEAVER, *Treasurer*
J. ALBERT BRIGGS, *Auditor*

* The *Development of Printing as an Art* handbook published in January 1906 shows J. Albert Briggs as treasurer.

1913–1914

DANIEL BERKELEY UPDIKE, *President*
HENRY LEWIS JOHNSON, *Vice-President*
C. C. LANE, *Secretary*
ROBERT SEAVER, *Treasurer*
W. F. LAMONT, *Auditor*

1914–1915

C. C. LANE, *President*
DOUGLAS G. FIELD, *Vice-President*
A. R. GETCHELL, *Secretary*
E. B. SHERRILL, *Treasurer*
ROBERT SEAVER, *Auditor*

1915–1916

C. C. LANE, *President*
A. R. GETCHELL, *Vice-President*
IRVING K. ANNABLE, *Secretary*
W. H. GREELEY,* *Treasurer*
A. A. STEWART, *Auditor*

1916–1917

C. F. WHITMARSH, *President*
ROBERT SEAVER, *Vice-President*
E. K. ROBINSON, *Secretary*
THOMAS TODD, *Treasurer*
WALT HARRIS, *Auditor*

1917–1918

ROBERT SEAVER, *President*
E. K. ROBINSON, *Vice-President*
W. M. STONE, *Secretary*
A. R. GETCHELL, *Treasurer*
WALT HARRIS, *Auditor*

1918–1919

ROBERT SEAVER, *President*
E. K. ROBINSON, *Vice-President*
W. M. STONE, *Secretary*
A. R. GETCHELL, *Treasurer*
W. F. LAMONT, *Auditor*

* C. F. Whitmarsh elected Treasurer December 1915 to replace W. H. Greeley, resigned.

1919–1920

HENRY LEWIS JOHNSON, *President*
L. P. CUDWORTH, *Vice-President*
W. M. STONE,* *Secretary*
WALT HARRIS, *Treasurer*
HERBERT FARRIER, *Auditor*

1920–1921

E. B. SHERRILL, *President*
WILLIAM A. DWIGGINS, *Vice-President*
W. M. STONE, *Secretary*
IRVING K. ANNABLE, *Treasurer*

1921–1922

E. B. SHERRILL, *President*
WILLIAM A. DWIGGINS, *Vice-President*
W. M. STONE, *Secretary*
IRVING K. ANNABLE, *Treasurer*

1922–1923

E. K. ROBINSON, *President*
W. F. LAMONT, *Vice-President*
IRVING K. ANNABLE, *Secretary*
THACHER NELSON, *Treasurer*
W. M. STONE, *Auditor*

1923–1924

E. K. ROBINSON, *President*
W. F. LAMONT, *Vice-President*
IRVING K. ANNABLE, *Secretary*
THACHER NELSON, *Treasurer*
W. M. STONE, *Auditor*

1924–1925

IRVING K. ANNABLE, *President*
JOHN C. HURD, *Vice-President*
LEWIS C. GANDY, *Secretary*
J. B. HOWLAND, *Treasurer*
HENRY LEWIS JOHNSON, *Auditor*

1925–1926

IRVING K. ANNABLE, *President*
JOHN C. HURD, *Vice-President*
CARROLL SMITH, *Secretary*
HORACE B. VAN EVEREN, *Treasurer*
CHARLES G. WELLS, *Auditor*

* David T. Pottinger elected Secretary January 1920 to replace W. M. Stone, resigned.

1926–1927
DAVID T. POTTINGER, *President*
T. B. HAPGOOD, *Vice-President*
JOHN C. HURD, *Secretary*
A. F. MACKAY, *Treasurer*

1927–1928
DAVID T. POTTINGER, *President*
JOHN C. HURD, *Vice-President*
THACHER NELSON, *Secretary*
A. F. MACKAY, *Treasurer*

1928–1929
JOHN C. HURD, *President*
THACHER NELSON, *Vice-President*
MAURICE BLACKMUR, *Secretary*
RAYMOND STRAWBRIDGE, *Treasurer*
AMOS WESTON, *Auditor*

1929–1930
JOHN C. HURD, *President*
THACHER NELSON, *Vice-President*
MAURICE BLACKMUR, *Secretary*
RAYMOND STRAWBRIDGE, *Treasurer*
AMOS WESTON, *Auditor*

1930–1931
THACHER NELSON, *President*
GEORGE PARKER WINSHIP, *Vice-President*
MAURICE BLACKMUR, *Secretary*
RAYMOND STRAWBRIDGE, *Treasurer*
AMOS WESTON, *Auditor*

1931–1932
THACHER NELSON, *President*
GEORGE PARKER WINSHIP, *Vice-President*
MAURICE BLACKMUR, *Secretary*
RAYMOND STRAWBRIDGE, *Treasurer*
AMOS WESTON, *Auditor*

1932–1933
G. S. HOWLAND, *President*
GEORGE PARKER WINSHIP, *Vice-President*
MAURICE BLACKMUR, *Secretary*
RAYMOND STRAWBRIDGE, *Treasurer*
AMOS WESTON, *Auditor*

1933–1934

G. S. HOWLAND, *President*
MAURICE BLACKMUR, *Vice-President*
DANIEL B. BIANCHI, *Secretary*
RAYMOND STRAWBRIDGE, *Treasurer*
AMOS WESTON, *Auditor*

1934–1935

HERBERT G. PORTER, *President*
ZOLTÁN HARASZTI, *Vice-President*
DANIEL B. BIANCHI, *Secretary*
RAYMOND STRAWBRIDGE, *Treasurer*
AMOS WESTON, *Auditor*

1935–1936

HERBERT G. PORTER, *President*
EDMUND W. STEVENS, *Vice-President*
DANIEL B. BIANCHI, *Secretary*
DONALD C. HAGAR, *Treasurer*
AMOS WESTON, *Auditor*

1936–1937

G. GEHMAN TAYLOR, *President*
GEORGE F. TRENHOLM, *Vice-President*
DANIEL B. BIANCHI, *Secretary*
DONALD C. HAGAR, *Treasurer*
AMOS WESTON, *Auditor*

1937–1938

G. GEHMAN TAYLOR, *President*
GEORGE F. TRENHOLM, *Vice-President*
FRANK LIGHTBOWN, *Secretary*
DONALD C. HAGAR, *Treasurer*
AMOS WESTON, *Auditor*

1938–1939

GEORGE F. TRENHOLM, *President*
WALTON C. ALLEN, *Vice-President*
FRANK LIGHTBOWN, *Secretary*
DONALD C. HAGAR, *Treasurer*
G. GEHMAN TAYLOR, *Auditor*

1939–1940

WALTON C. ALLEN, *President*
WATSON M. GORDON, *Vice-President*
FRANK LIGHTBOWN, *Secretary*
DONALD C. HAGAR, *Treasurer*
G. GEHMAN TAYLOR, *Auditor*

1940–1941

CARLTON M. STRONG, *President*
ARTHUR WILLIAMS, *Vice-President*
FRANK LIGHTBOWN, *Secretary*
DONALD C. HAGAR, *Treasurer*
WALTON C. ALLEN, *Auditor*

1941–1942

CARLTON M. STRONG, *President*
ARTHUR WILLIAMS, *Vice-President*
FRANK LIGHTBOWN, *Secretary*
DONALD C. HAGAR, *Treasurer*
WALTON C. ALLEN, *Auditor*

1942–1943

ARTHUR WILLIAMS, *President*
HOWARD WALLINGFORD, *Vice-President*
FRANK LIGHTBOWN, *Secretary*
DONALD C. HAGAR, *Treasurer*
CARLTON M. STRONG, *Auditor*

1943–1944

HOWARD WALLINGFORD, *President*
HARRY F. HOWARD, *Vice-President*
FRANK LIGHTBOWN, *Secretary*
DONALD C. HAGAR, *Treasurer*
ARTHUR F. WILLIAMS, *Auditor*

1944–1945

HARRY F. HOWARD, *President*
RONALD W. MURRAY, *Vice-President*
FRANK LIGHTBOWN, *Secretary*
DONALD C. HAGAR, *Treasurer*
HOWARD WALLINGFORD, *Auditor*

1945–1946

RONALD W. MURRAY, *President*
MILLARD D. TAYLOR, *Vice-President*
HORACE L. ARNOLD, *Secretary*
WALTER W. ANNABLE, *Treasurer*
HARRY F. HOWARD, *Auditor*

1946–1947

RONALD W. MURRAY, *President*
MILLARD D. TAYLOR, *Vice-President*
HORACE L. ARNOLD, *Secretary*
WALTER W. ANNABLE, *Treasurer*
HARRY F. HOWARD, *Auditor*

1947–1948

MILLARD D. TAYLOR, *President*
FRANK LIGHTBOWN, *Vice-President*
FRANCIS X. DUGGAN, *Secretary*
WALTER W. ANNABLE, *Treasurer*
RONALD W. MURRAY, *Auditor*

1948–1949

MILLARD D. TAYLOR, *President*
FRANK LIGHTBOWN, *Vice-President*
FRANCIS X. DUGGAN, *Secretary*
WALTER W. ANNABLE, *Treasurer*
RONALD W. MURRAY, *Auditor*

1949–1950

FRANK LIGHTBOWN, *President*
BURTON L. STRATTON, *Vice-President*
A. BRADLEE EMMONS, *Secretary*
WALTER W. ANNABLE, *Treasurer*
MILLARD D. TAYLOR, *Auditor*

1950–1951

BURTON L. STRATTON, *President*
DANIEL B. BIANCHI, *Vice-President*
A. BRADLEE EMMONS, *Secretary*
WALTER W. ANNABLE, *Treasurer*
FRANK LIGHTBOWN, *Auditor*

1951–1952

DANIEL B. BIANCHI, *President*
HARRY L. GAGE, *Vice-President*
MORTON H. BAKER, *Secretary*
THOMAS TODD, JR., *Treasurer*
BURTON L. STRATTON, *Auditor*

1952–1953

ALBERT R. GETCHELL, *President*
CHARLES H. GUSHEE, *Vice-President*
MORTON H. BAKER, *Secretary*
THOMAS TODD, JR., *Treasurer*
DANIEL B. BIANCHI, *Auditor*

1953–1954

CHARLES H. GUSHEE, *President*
GEORGE MARSH, *Vice-President*
THEODORE C. CRAWFORD, *Secretary*
HAROLD LIGHTBOWN, *Treasurer*
ALBERT R. GETCHELL, *Auditor*

1954–1955
ROLLO G. SILVER, *President*
ALAN STEPHENS, *Vice-President*
CHARLES W. BOWKER, *Secretary*
HAROLD LIGHTBOWN, *Treasurer*
CHARLES H. GUSHEE, *Auditor*

Terms and Symbols Used in the
Register of Members

Members are active members unless otherwise noted.

Abbreviations:

a before a date	ante
c before a date	circa
†	deceased

Dates are used as follows:

1915–	election in 1915 continuing until the present
1915	election 1915, separation date unknown
*a*1915–1928	election before 1915, exact date unknown, and continuing until 1928
*c*1915– †	election about 1915, exact date unknown, and continuing until death of member
list	name on a single membership list, exact date of election and separation unknown

Register of Members

M. A. ABBOTT 1914 *list*

ARTHUR S. ALLEN 1905–1906 *exhibit committee*

WALTON C. ALLEN 1936–

WINTHROP AMES 1905–1906 *exhibit committee*

JAMES A. ANDERSON *non-resident a*1914–

JEROME S. ANDERSON, III 1951–

IRVING K. ANNABLE *a*1914– †

WALTER W. ANNABLE *a*1923–

FRED ANTHOENSEN *non-resident* 1936–1938

E. P. ARCHIBALD 1923–1924 *list*

HORACE L. ARNOLD 1939–

HENRY TURNER BAILEY *charter* †

J. AUSTIN BAILEY 1945–

MORTON H. BAKER 1949–

SAMUEL F. BAKER 1942–1944

EDMUND J. BARNARD 1946–1951

PAUL H. BARTER 1949–

ALFRED BARTLETT *charter*– †

BRAINARD L. BATES 1914 *list*

REUEL W. BEACH 1934–1946

PAUL A. BENNETT *non-resident* 1940–

THEODORE BERGER 1916–1917 *list*

ANSELMO BIANCHI 1914 *list* †

DANIEL B. BIANCHI 1933–

JOHN BIANCHI *a*1912–1949

MORRIS G. BISHOP 1915

W. J. BISHOP 1917–1918 *list*

MAURICE A. BLACKMUR *a*1925–1942

IRWIN L. BOGIN *non-resident* 1937–1941

EDWARD E. BOURGET *a*1927–1928

CHARLES W. BOWKER 1944–

R. BOWSER *student* 1914 *list*

JOSEPH BRADFORD *non-resident* 1936–1950

JOHN HOWIE BREWER 1936–1938

J. ALBERT BRIGGS 1905

FRANK C. BROWN *a*1909

DAVENPORT BROWN 1925–

HENRY LEWIS BULLEN *a*1917 *honorary* 1934– †

JACKSON BURKE *non-resident* 1954–

LESLIE S. BURNELL 1941–1947

RANDAL C. BURRELL 1937–

LUTHER T. CALKINS *non-resident* 1915

CHARLES R. CAPON *a*1916– †

I. W. CARPENTER, JR. *student* 1915–1916 *list*

MELBERT B. CARY, JR. *non-resident* 1929–1937

J. H. CHAPIN 1909

N. B. CLARK *student* 1915–1916 *list*

JAMES G. CLARKE 1927–1939 †

DONALD H. CLAUSS *non-resident* 1937–

W. J. COLBY *a*1914–1914

W. ARTHUR COLE *non-resident* 1915–

THEODORE R. CRAWFORD 1944–

HARRY R. CROCKETT 1914 *list*

LUTHER P. CUDWORTH *a*1913

EVERETT R. CURRIER *non-resident* 1916

JOHN B. CURRY 1928– †

FRANK CUSHING 1936–1945

RAYMOND B. DAIGLE 1943–

JOSEPH J. DALLAS 1933–1936

JOHN COTTON DANA *non-resident* 1914 *list*

GEORGE W. DAVIDSON 1944–

WARREN G. DAVIS 1930

HERMAN DEAN 1939–1942

DONALD R. DE LORIEA *a*1913

ADDIS W. DEMPSEY 1941–

THEODORE LOW DE VINNE *honorary* 1905– †

JOSEPH P. DONOVAN 1936–

ROBERT L. DOTHARD *non-resident* 1942–

FRANK T. DUFFEY 1933–1937

FRANCIS X. DUGGAN 1946–

REUBEN DUNSFORD 1936–1947

WILLIAM ADDISON DWIGGINS *a*1912 *honorary* 1924–

JAMES K. EATON 1923–1924 *list*

ROBERT S. ELLIOTT 1940–1943

A. W. ELSON *a*1913– †

GEORGE EMMEL 1916–1917 *list*

A. BRADLEE EMMONS 1937–

ARTHUR A. ENGLISH 1950–
ROYAL B. FARNUM 1927
CLARENCE E. FARRAR 1937–1941
HERBERT FARRIER 1916–
HARRY M. FAUNCE 1937–
DOUGLAS G. FIELD 1913
A. W. FINLAY 1937–1949 †
OTTO FLEISCHNER *charter*
RICHARD W. FLEWELLING 1939–
DEAN G. FREEMAN 1916
GEORGE FRENCH *charter*
C. K. FULLER 1923–1924 *list*
HARRY L. GAGE 1948–
LEWIS C. GANDY *a*1913 *honorary* 1937– †
BURTON GARBER 1939–
WILLIE C. GARDNER *student* 1915–1916 *list*
EDWIN F. GAY *honorary* 1913– †
W. ELLSWORTH GEIST 1948–
ALBERT R. GETCHELL *a*1910–
WALTER GILLISS *honorary* 1913 †
EDWIN GINN 1923–1924 *list* †
BERTRAM G. GOODHUE *non-resident a*1914–1924 †
CHARLES E. GOODSPEED *a*1914–1915 †
EUGENE H. GORDON 1941–
WATSON M. GORDON 1929–
FREDERIC W. GOUDY *non-resident* 1916 *honorary* – †
GEORGE GRADY *non-resident* 1944–1947
RUTH SHEPARD GRANNISS *honorary* 1939– †
P. B. GRAY *student* 1915–1916 *list*
W. H. GREELEY *charter honorary* 1943– †
HERBERT GREGSON 1923–1924 *list*
WILLIAM P. GREULING 1942–1948
LINCOLN C. GRUSH 1938–1943
CHARLES H. GUSHEE 1942–
EDMOND BYRNE HACKETT *non-resident* 1909
DONALD C. HAGAR 1933–
ABRAHAM HAMBURG 1927–1939
THEODORE BROWN HAPGOOD, JR. 1905– †
ZOLTÁN HARASZTI 1934–1941
GEORGE L. HARDING *student* 1915–1916 *list*
WALT HARRIS *a*1914–1928 †
LEWIS HATCH 1909

CARL H. HEINTZEMANN *charter* †
CHARLES HEINTZEMANN 1934–1950
GEORGE A. HEINTZEMANN 1914 *list*
DEAN HOCKING 1951–
E. F. HODGINS 1927
PHILIP HOFER 1939–
PHILIP C. HOLDEN 1938–
AMOR HOLLINGSWORTH *a*1911–1938
AMOR HOLLINGSWORTH, JR. 1938–
ARTHUR T. HOWARD 1949–
HARRY F. HOWARD 1942–
JAMES HOWARD 1943–1949 †
F. S. HOWE *student* 1914 *list*
GERALD S. HOWLAND 1913–1937 †
J. B. HOWLAND *a*1924
SHEPARD HOWLAND 1914
E. HAROLD HUGO *non-resident* 1949–
DARD HUNTER 1941–1943
DARD HUNTER, JR. 1941–1943
JOHN COOLIDGE HURD *a*1923–
JAMES E. INNES 1917–1918 *list*
ADRIAN J. IORIO 1914–1939
P. L. JACKSON *student* 1915–1916 *list*
ELMER M. JENKINS 1949–
HENRY LEWIS JOHNSON *charter honorary* 1934– †
A. MARSHALL JONES *a*1923–1928
BURTON J. JONES, JR. 1949–
FRANK R. JORDAN 1924
FRANKLIN I. JORDAN 1927
WILLARD K. JOYCE 1951–
ALFRED V. JULES 1944–1945
GEORGE A. JUST 1929–1930 *list*
EDWARD A. KARR 1945–
GEORGE F. KELLEY 1942–
HENRY WATSON KENT *non-resident a*1914 *honorary* 1939 †
NEWELL G. KEYES 1928–1937
WARREN S. KILBURN 1916 †
SIDNEY A. KIMBER 1905–
R. B. KINGMAN *non-resident* 1914 *list*
ARNOLD J. KIRSHEN 1949–
MAX S. KIRSHEN 1947–
FRANK KNOX 1930 †

HARRY LYMAN KOOPMAN 1909 *honorary* 1934– †

W. F. LAMONT *a*1913

CHARLES CHESTER LANE *a*1908

JOHN ALDEN LEE 1905–1915

BARNARD J. LEWIS *a*1914–1936

FRANK LIGHTBOWN 1935–

HAROLD LIGHTBOWN 1952–

JOHN MASON LINCOLN 1938–1944

MELVIN W. LOOS *non-resident* 1944–1950

RAYMOND H. LUFKIN *non-resident* 1934–

GORDON LUNDGREN *non-resident* 1943–1946

W. E. LUNDQUIST *student* 1914 *and* 1915–1916 *lists*

J. G. MACDONOUGH *student* 1914 *list*

A. F. MACKAY *charter* †

FRANK J. MADDEN 1938–

CHARLES A. MAHONEY 1950–

FRED W. MAIN *non-resident* 1937–1938 †

GEORGE MARSH 1941–

GEORGE R. MARVIN *a*1923–1936 †

PHILIP J. MC ATEER 1936–

JOHN O. C. MC CRILLIS 1941–1949

JOHN H. MC CULLOUGH 1932–1937

J. H. HORACE MC FARLAND *non-resident c*1910– †

JAMES W. MC FARLANE 1942–

WILLIAM E. MC FARLIN, JR. 1954–

HAROLD G. MC MENNAMIN 1944–

RICHMOND MAYO-SMITH *student* 1915–1916 *list*

FREDERIC G. MELCHER *honorary* 1952

WILLIAM F. MEYER, JR. 1952–

EDWARD L. MORSS *a*1915

R. B. MORSS *a*1913

NORMAN T. A. MUNDER *non-resident* 1914 *list*

ALBERT C. MURRAY 1940–

RONALD W. MURRAY 1933–

DONALD MYRICK *student* 1915–1916 *list*

RAY NASH *non-resident* 1940–

THACHER NELSON *a*1922– †

FREDERICK D. NICHOLS *charter*

CHARLES ELIOT NORTON *honorary* 1905– †

D. B. OGDEN *a*1913–1914

WILLIAM DANA ORCUTT *charter honorary* 1938– †

FORREST W. ORR 1937–

JOHN H. ORRALL, JR. 1954–
CHARLES A. PAGE 1925–1926 *list*
R. T. PEARL 1915 †
W. HARRISON PERRY 1940–
STARR MAC G. PIERCE 1923–1924 *list*
ANTHONY J. PHILPOTT *a*1913 †
C. A. PINKHAM *a*1916–1936 †
H. W. PLIMPTON *student* 1915–1916 *list* †
GEORGE T. PLOWMAN 1916– †
P. W. PORRITT *student* 1915–1916 *list*
HERBERT G. PORTER *a*1927– †
DAVID THOMAS POTTINGER *c*1919–1947
L. A. RANKIN 1914 *list*
ERNEST RAPA 1954–
FIORE A. RAPA 1937–
JOHN RAYMOND 1944–1949
SHEPARD A. RAYMOND 1924
WALTER E. REID 1917–1918 *list*
VERN H. RICHARDS 1940–
DONALD RICHARDSON 1949–
C. H. ROBERTS 1914 *list*
RICHARD F. ROBERTSON 1940–
W. FORBES ROBERTSON 1917–1941
EDWARD K. ROBINSON 1909–
BRUCE ROGERS *charter honorary* 1924–
CARL PURINGTON ROLLINS *non-resident* 1909 *honorary*
    1934–
GUSTAVE NILS ROUBOUND 1952–
E. L. ROWLAND *student* 1914 *list*
WILLIAM E. RUDGE *non-resident* 1942–
RUDOLPH RUZICKA 1948 *honorary* 1952–
HENRY N. SAWYER 1937–1939
DONALD SCOTT *non-resident* 1909–1927
ROBERT SEAVER *a*1912 †
BENJAMIN F. SHERBOW *non-resident* 1914 *list*
CLARENCE E. SHERMAN *non-resident* 1939–
EDGAR B. SHERRILL *a*1913–1937
JOHN R. SHULTZ 1928–1936
DAVID SILVE *non-resident* *a*1923–1927
ROLLO G. SILVER 1952–
CARL G. SMITH *a*1923–
CARROLL D. SMITH *a*1915–

MORGAN SMITH 1950–
ROGER DAY SMITH 1905 †
T. P. SMITH 1925–1926 *list*
WALTER A. SMITH 1947– †
JOHN S. SMYTH 1942–
R. M. SPENCER 1930
W. E. SPURRIER 1913
ALAN STEPHENS 1939–
EDMUND W. STEVENS *a*1927–
FRANK H. STEVENS, JR. 1939– †
HERMON W. STEVENS 1923–1924 *list*
ALEXANDER A. STEWART *charter*– †
EDWIN T. STIGER 1905
RODERICK D. STINEHOUR *non-resident* 1952–
WALTER M. STONE *student* 1914, 1916
BURTON L. STRATTON 1948–
RAYMOND C. STRAWBRIDGE 1927–1939
CARLTON M. STRONG 1936–
ALLEN W. SUMNER 1905
MILTON SUNDERLAND 1928
LINDSAY SWIFT 1905– †
G. GEHMAN TAYLOR 1927–
H. H. TAYLOR *student* 1914 *list*
J. G. TAYLOR 1914 *list*
MILLARD D. TAYLOR 1937–
C. B. THOMPSON 1914 *list*
LOVELL THOMPSON 1937–1941
ROBERT F. THOMPSON 1942–
GEORGE P. TILTON *a*1909–1915
THOMAS TODD 1909–
THOMAS TODD JR. 1948–
ANDREW J. TORRIELLI 1948–
GEORGE F. TRENHOLM 1917–
DANIEL BERKELEY UPDIKE *charter honorary* 1934– †
HORACE B. VAN EVEREN *a*1925–1927
FREDERICK K. VROOM *student* 1914 *list*, 1917–1918 *list*
RALPH J. WAITE 1938–
C. HOWARD WALKER *charter* †
FRITZ WALKER 1954–
HOWARD WALLINGFORD 1935–
ROBERT WALLINGFORD 1951–
PERRY WALTON 1909 *honorary* 1937– †

BERTON G. WANDS 1927–1937 †

L. M. WASHBURN *student* 1915–1916 *list*

E. J. WATSON 1915

HANSON H. WEBSTER 1909

JOSEPH CLEMENT WEISS 1949–

CHARLES G. WELLS 1909 †

EDGAR F. WELLS *non-resident* 1923–1924 *list*

AMOS E. WESTON 1915– †

HARRY H. WETHERALD *non-resident* 1944–

WILLIAM BOND WHEELWRIGHT *a*1908–1943

HERBERT H. WHITE *charter*

FREDERIC ALLEN WHITING 1905

C. F. WHITMARSH *a*1911 †

ARTHUR F. WILLIAMS 1937– †

ROBERT W. WILLIAMSON, JR. 1945–

CHARLES A. WILSON 1925–1926 *list*

WILLIAM K. WILSON 1929

GEORGE PARKER WINSHIP *c*1909 *honorary* 1939– †

LAWRENCE COUNSELMAN WROTH *non-resident* 1930 *honorary* 1934–

EMERSON G. WULLING *non-resident* 1924

Index

THE SOCIETY OF PRINTERS is deeply indebted to all those participating in the production of this volume, and through its Publication Committee extends its most sincere appreciation to all contributors.

In particular, special thanks go to the following: Mr. Bruce Rogers for his typographic arrangement and design; Miss Veronica Ruzicka for special permission to use a reproduction of one of her paste paper designs on the cover; Miss Eleanor Bates for extremely helpful editorial assistance; The Riverside Press, Cambridge, Massachusetts, for the typesetting and presswork; The Meriden Gravure Company, Meriden, Connecticut, for the printing of the illustrations and the cover; Curtis Paper Company, Newark, Delaware, and Stevens-Nelson Hobson Miller, Inc., Charlestown, Massachusetts, for the Curtis Rag Natural paper; and Robert Burlen & Son, Boston, Massachusetts, for the binding. The jacket design, adapted from the cover of the Society's *Miscellany*, is the work of George F. Trenholm. The jacket was printed by A. T. Howard Company, Boston, Massachusetts.

The Committee is also grateful to the officers of the Society for their patience and sympathetic understanding during the progress of the work and especially to the presidents during the last three terms, Messrs. Albert R. Getchell, Charles H. Gushee, and Rollo G. Silver. Last, but by no means least, we here acknowledge with profound thanks the generosity of the Harvard University Press in publishing this edition at modest cost and in taking so large an interest in furthering the aims of the Society.

The Fiftieth Anniversary Publication Committee

This book was written to commemorate
The Fiftieth Anniversary of the Society of Printers
Designed by Bruce Rogers

Fifteen hundred copies printed

THE SOCIETY OF PRINTERS: FOR THE STUDY AND
ADVANCEMENT OF THE ART OF PRINTING: BOSTON

SP

May 4, 1905.

Dear Sir:

There will be a meeting of
this Society at the Boston Athletic
Association, Exeter St., on Monday,
May 8.   Dinner will be served at 6.30
P.M., at $1.25 a plate.

Mr. Otto Fleischner will speak
on the proposed publication relating to
"Bibliography of Printing."   Reports
will be received and plans made for the
proposed Franklin Exhibition in 1906.

Enclosed please find card for
reply.

Very truly yours,

Henry L. Johnson

Secretary.

Mr. D. Berkeley Updike,
       232 Summer St., Boston.

1   MEETING NOTICE, DATED MAY 4, 1905, ON THE NEW OFFICIAL STATIONERY

THE DEVELOPMENT
OF PRINTING AS AN ART

A HANDBOOK
OF THE EXHIBITION IN HONOR OF
THE BI-CENTENARY OF FRANK-
LIN'S BIRTH HELD AT THE
BOSTON PUBLIC LIBRARY
UNDER THE AUSPICES
OF THE SOCIETY
OF PRINTERS

SP

PUBLICATIONS OF THE SOCIETY, NUMBER II
BOSTON, MASSACHUSETTS
JANUARY 1 TO 29, 1906

B

A

2   EARLIEST PUBLICATIONS: (A) HANDBOOK OF THE SOCIETY, JUNE 1905; (B) EXHIBITION CATALOGUE

B

Three
Illustrated Lectures
under auspices of the
Society of Printers
On Thursday Evenings
at 8 o'clock

January 30
**Modern Printing Establishments
and their Output
By Henry Lewis Johnson**

February 27
**Distinctive Types of American
Illustration
By Charles H. Caffin**

March 12
**Design and Color in Printing
By Henry Turner Bailey**

No Tickets are Required

PROPOSAL FOR MEMBERSHIP
.·.
THE SOCIETY OF PRINTERS
FOR THE STUDY AND ADVANCEMENT OF
THE ART OF PRINTING

4 JOY STREET
BOSTON

A

3   (A) MEMBERSHIP PROPOSAL FORM, 1905; (B) ANNOUNCEMENT OF PUBLIC LIBRARY LECTURES, 1908 SERIES

Society of Printers

Annual Meeting
Nov. 10, 1908

In accordance with the provisions of the constitution a Council of nine members was elected

Henry L. Johnson   Otto Fleischner
W. H. Greeley   W. B. Wheelwright
J. A. Briggs   Henry T. Bailey
W. D. Orcutt   C. C. Lane
D. B. Updike

A question was raised as to the most convenient night for holding the regular monthly meetings and it was —
Voted that hereafter the monthly meetings be held on the first Monday of each month

The previous vote of the Society authorizing the publication of a pamphlet was brought to the attention of the members and it was:—
Voted that the necessary material be brought together as soon as possible and turned over to Mr Bailey to edit for publication

The question of establishing a jury to pass on specimens of work

THE SOCIETY
OF
PRINTERS

SP

NEW YORK VISIT
MCMIX

5   SOUVENIR MENU OF THE NEW YORK VISIT OF NOVEMBER 1909

PRINTING CONNECTED WITH THE SOCIETY
OF PRINTERS, BOSTON.

Society of Printers New York visit. Menu of dinner at The Players
Club with autographs of members. 1909.

Keepsake Nov. 11. 1913. Printed by the Merrymount Press (Walker Circular?)

Circular of the Plantin Press distributed at a dinner of the
Society of Printers, July 1913, Printed at the McGrath & Woodley
Press.

Keepsake of the Society of Printers, March 4, 1913, with signatures
of persons present. Consists of Standard Trade Terms used by
Photo-Engravers. Arranged by C. F. Whitmarsh, Cambridge.

Keepsake of the Society of Printers, April 22, 1913. Printed and
designed by W. A. Dwiggins. (Bodoni).

Keepsake of the Society of Printers, May 20, 1913. Prepared by Henry
Lewis Johnson. (Colour Printing).

Keepsake of the Society of Printers, October 23, 1913. Printed by
the Seaver-Howland Press. (The Yarn of the Nancy Bell).

Keepsake of the Society of Printers, November 13, 1914. Prepared by
D. B. Updike The Merrymount Press. (Walpole).

Society of Printers Reports and List of Members, 1914.

Keepsake of the Society of Printers, February 24, 1914. Printed by
Addison C. Getchell & Son, Boston. (Baskerville).

Keepsake of the Society of Printers, March 25, 1914. Printed by the
Athenaeum Press, Cambridge. (Plantin).

Keepsake of the Society of Printers, April 28, 1914. Printed by the
Riverside Press, Cambridge. (Goodspeed's Talk on One Hundred Years
of American Pictorial Illustrations).

Keepsake of the Society of Printers, May 28, 1914. Printed by the
Christian Science Publishing Society. (Didot).

Keepsake of the Society of Printers, October 15, 1914. Printed on
the occasion of a talk given by Mr. C. E. Lauriat, Jr. on the
Leipzig Book Show.

Keepsake of the Society of Printers, November 10, 1914. Printed at
the Heintzemann Press, Boston. (Ivins talk.)

Keepsake of the Society of Printers, January 7, 1915. Printed by
Addison C. Getchell & Son, Boston. (Howard Walker's address).

6   FIRST PAGE OF THE UPDIKE SCRAPBOOK, 'MERRYMOUNT COLLECTION XVII'

An Informal Dinner

Tendered to

C. C. LANE *(President)*
HENRY LEWIS JOHNSON
CARROLL D. SMITH
L. J. CALKINS
ADRIAN J. IORIO
A. J. PHILPOTT
R. A. PHILPOTT
CHARLES G. WELLS
E. L. MORSS
JAMES A. ANDERSON
EDGAR B. SHERRILL
ALBERT R. GETCHELL
GEORGE P. TILTON
J. H. McSHANE
E. BYRNE HACKETT
BRAINARD L. BATES
GEORGE PARKER WINSHIP
BENJAMIN F. SHERBOW
DONALD SCOTT

a delegation of

THE SOCIETY OF PRINTERS OF BOSTON

by THE AMERICAN INSTITUTE OF
GRAPHIC ARTS, *at the National
Arts Club, New York, May 25th, 1915*

WILLIAM ADDISON DWIGGINS, DESIGNER
HINGHAM, BOSTON   26 Lime St

Il faut cultiver notre Jardin

TELEPHONE
HAYMARKET 1693-2

Dec 23 1915

Dear Alfred:—

The Society of Printers at their last meeting appointed a committee — Mr. Updike, Mr. Winship and myself — to send you a Christmas card for the Society. I am mailing it to you this P.M., registered, and hope it gets through safely.

The members asked after you and took your address and you may get a few cards from them personally.

Alas, I have not made one for myself this year. I have been buried as usual just before the holidays and have not had time to sleep!

After Christmas I hope to be able to see you, will at least write a connected letter.

Your news of your health in your last was encouraging. I hope that it may mean an early "pardon".

Haven't had time to get in touch with Miss Birdsall. No news from Palmer for months. Phillips is back on his old job on the Herald.

Will said you a "Fabulist" as soon as I have time to address one.

As Merry a Christmas as it is possible to have under the circumstance. Not so dung-blasted merry, I fear! But we are thinking of you.

Sincerely, Bill.

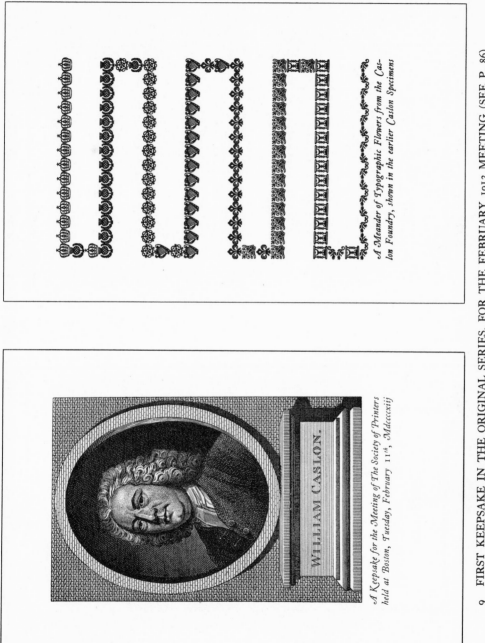

A Keepsake for the Meeting of The Society of Printers
held at Boston, Tuesday, February 11th, Mdcccxiij

WILLIAM CASLON.

A Meander of Typographic Flowers from the Caslon Foundry, shown in the earlier Caslon Specimens

9   FIRST KEEPSAKE IN THE ORIGINAL SERIES, FOR THE FEBRUARY 1913 MEETING (SEE P. 86)

STANDARD
TRADE TERMS USED BY
PHOTO-ENGRAVERS

THE terms used by photo-engravers are not always clearly understood by those who have occasion to order illustrations, nor have they been as carefully standardized as those applying to some of the other branches of printing. The accompanying list is presented with a view of familiarizing members of The Society of Printers with the standard trade terms recently adopted by the International Association of Photo-Engravers. It is hoped that the universal adoption of these will avoid confusion and be of help to the man who orders illustrations as well as to the firm producing them.

HALF-TONE — SQUARE PLATE. — A half-tone in which the outside edges are rectangular and parallel, may be with or without single black line border.

HALF-TONE — OUTLINED. — A half-tone with the background outside of the object entirely cut away, leaving a definite edge without shading or vignetting.

HALF-TONE — VIGNETTED. — A half-tone in which one or more of the edges of the object are shaded from dark tones to pure white.

HALF-TONE — OUTLINED and VIGNETTED. — A half-tone in which part of the background is cut away and part vignetted.

CUT. — Never use this obsolete term, as it does not apply to the photo-engraving business; use the terms "engravings," or "plates."

STANDARD
TRADE TERMS USED BY
PHOTO-ENGRAVERS

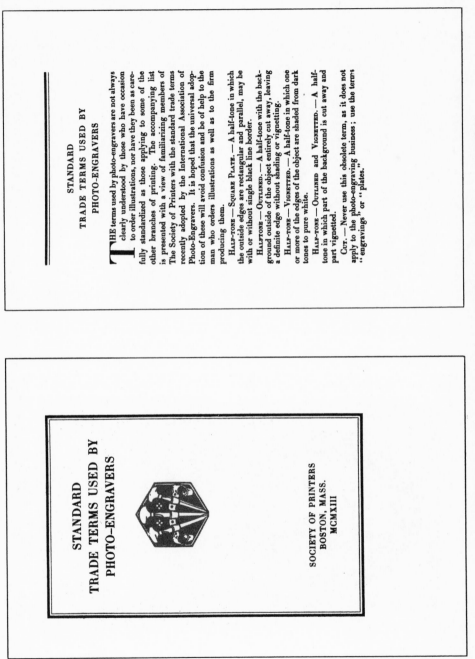

SOCIETY OF PRINTERS
BOSTON, MASS.
MCMXIII

11 D. B. UPDIKE'S COPY OF THE MARCH 1913 KEEPSAKE, SHOWING AUTOGRAPHS (SEE NOTE 64)

Seventy-five copies printed at the White Elephant, Hingham, the first impressions from that establishment

WAS SOLL ICH

DAMIT THUN?

SP

A Keepsake in honour of Giambattista Bodoni, printed for the Meeting of the Society of Printers held on Tuesday, April Twenty-second, Nineteen hundred & thirteen

The Society of Printers at its meeting on May 20, 1913, will greet Mr. John Cotton Dana as a fellow member and as one of the most influential men in the interests of this Society: „For the study and advancement of the art of printing."

The subject of the evening will be The Modern Revival of Printing in Germany, by Mr. Dana, and there will be an interesting collection of specimens of typical German typography.

Keepsake of the evening prepared by Henry Lewis Johnson

13 KEEPSAKE PREPARED BY H. L. JOHNSON FOR THE MAY 1913 MEETING

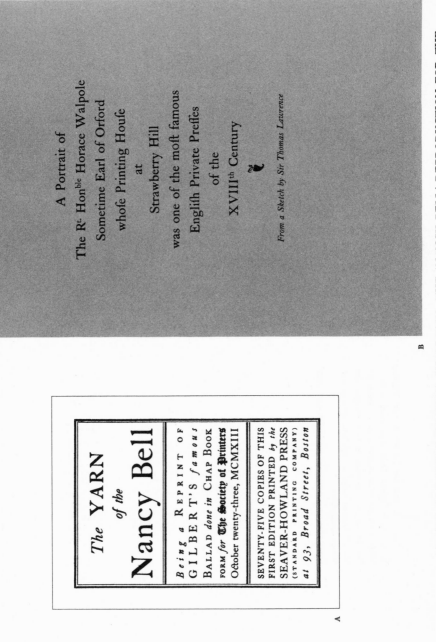

A Portrait of
The Rᵗ Honᵇˡᵉ Horace Walpole
Sometime Earl of Orford
whofe Printing Houfe
at
Strawberry Hill
was one of the moft famous
Englifh Private Preffes
of the
XVIIIᵗʰ Century

From a Sketch by Sir Thomas Lawrence

The YARN
of the
Nancy Bell

Being a REPRINT OF
GILBERT'S *famous*
BALLAD *done in* CHAP BOOK
FORM *for* The Society of Printers
October twenty-three, MCMXIII

SEVENTY-FIVE COPIES OF THIS
FIRST EDITION PRINTED *by the*
SEAVER-HOWLAND PRESS
(STANDARD PRINTING COMPANY)
at 93, Broad Street, Boston

A

B

14 (A) ONE OF ROBERT SEAVER'S CHAPBOOKS, THE 'NANCY BELL' REPRODUCTION FOR THE
NOVEMBER 1913 MEETING; (B) COVER FOR A WALPOLE PORTRAIT

A page from "La Vera Arte de lo Excellente Scrivere", G. A. Tagliente, Venice, 1524; copied for the Society of Printers on the occasion of their meeting of December 29, 1913, at which Mr W. A. Dwiggins and Mr T. B. Hapgood talked of Early Writing-books and Modern Calligraphy. Seventy-five copies printed by The Heintzemann Press.

15 A PAGE COPIED FROM TAGLIENTE FOR THE DECEMBER 1913 MEETING

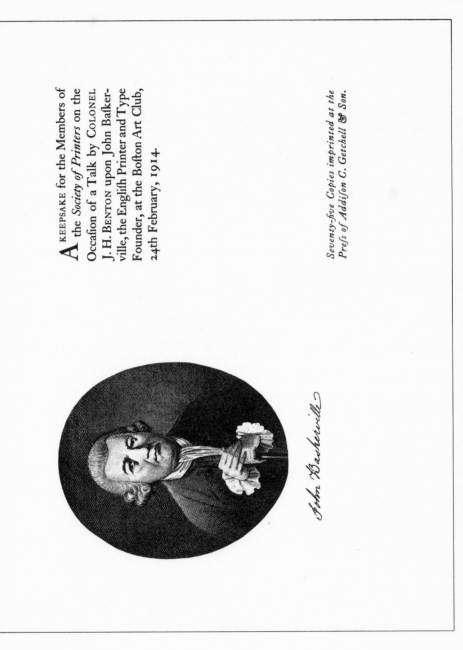

A KEEPSAKE for the Members of the *Society of Printers* on the Occasion of a Talk by COLONEL J. H. BENTON upon John Bakerville, the Englifh Printer and Type Founder, at the Bofton Art Club, 24th February, 1914.

Seventy-five Copies imprinted at the Prefs of Addifon C. Getchell & Son.

John Baskerville

THE SOCIETY OF PRINTERS
BOSTON

• •

GENTLEMEN: I have the honour to submit herewith my annual report as President of the Society of Printers.

Since last year some changes have been made in the Constitution of the Society. These aim to form a government more representative of our membership: and accordingly the nomination of officers is no longer confined to members of the council. It has also been provided that the annual reports of the president and treasurer shall be printed and sent to all members. In the discretion of the council, that paper which is voted by our membership to be the most interesting or valuable of those delivered during the twelve months previous to the annual meeting may be printed and similarly distributed. A few copies will be for sale.

The By-Laws of the Society have also been amended so that the duties of the treasurer are more clearly defined. Non-resident members have been placed in a class by themselves, their fee being reduced to half that of resident members, thus giving an opportunity for a larger active resident membership. The eleven vacancies caused by this arrangement have all been filled. The resident membership of the Society now numbers forty-seven and the non-resident, eleven; leaving but three vacancies in the resident membership list, which by the Constitution is limited to fifty.

During the past year, by vote of the council, a grant amounting to $262.53 was made toward the support of the course on the Technique of Printing in the Graduate School of Business Administration at Harvard University, for which acknowledgement was received from the Treasurer, and a vote of thanks from the President and Fellows of the University. It has given us much pleasure to welcome to the Society the members of the class who are taking this

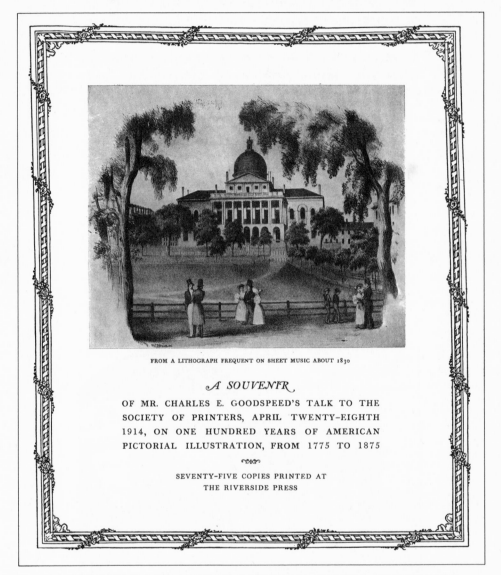

FROM A LITHOGRAPH FREQUENT ON SHEET MUSIC ABOUT 1830

A SOUVENIR

OF MR. CHARLES E. GOODSPEED'S TALK TO THE
SOCIETY OF PRINTERS, APRIL TWENTY–EIGHTH
1914, ON ONE HUNDRED YEARS OF AMERICAN
PICTORIAL ILLUSTRATION, FROM 1775 TO 1875

SEVENTY-FIVE COPIES PRINTED AT
THE RIVERSIDE PRESS

18 SOUVENIR OF THE TALK ON AMERICAN PICTORIAL ILLUSTRATION
BY CHARLES E. GOODSPEED

PRINTED ON THE OCCASION OF A TALK GIVEN BY MR. C. E. LAURIAT, JR., OF BOSTON, BEFORE THE SOCIETY OF PRINTERS, ON THURSDAY EVENING, OCTOBER FIFTEENTH, 1914, DESCRIBING HIS VISIT TO THE INTERNATIONAL EXPOSITION DEVOTED TO THE BOOK, AND TO THE ARTS AND INDUSTRIES CONNECTED WITH ITS PRODUCTION, HELD DURING THE PAST SUMMER AT LEIPZIG.

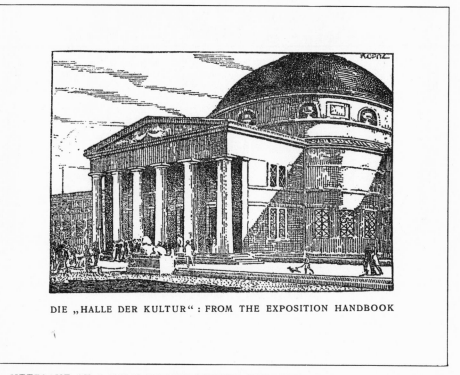

DIE „HALLE DER KULTUR" : FROM THE EXPOSITION HANDBOOK

19 KEEPSAKE OF A TALK ON THE LEIPZIG EXPOSITION BY C. E. LAURIAT, JR.

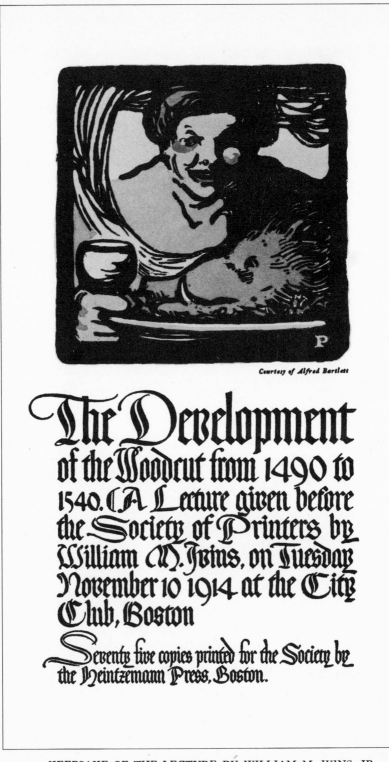

Courtesy of Alfred Bartlett

The Development
of the Woodcut from 1490 to
1540. A Lecture given before
the Society of Printers by
William M. Ivins, on Tuesday
November 10 1914 at the City
Club, Boston

Seventy five copies printed for the Society by
the Heintzemann Press, Boston.

HISTORIC·ORNAMENT
IN·ITS·RELATION
TO·PRINTING

BY

C·HOWARD·WALKER
LECTURER·AND·WRITER
ON·DECORATION·AND·ORNAMENT
⁂
BOSTON·CITY·CLUB
JANUARY·7·1915

21 DESIGN BY WALT HARRIS FOR THE C. HOWARD WALKER MEETING,
JANUARY 1915

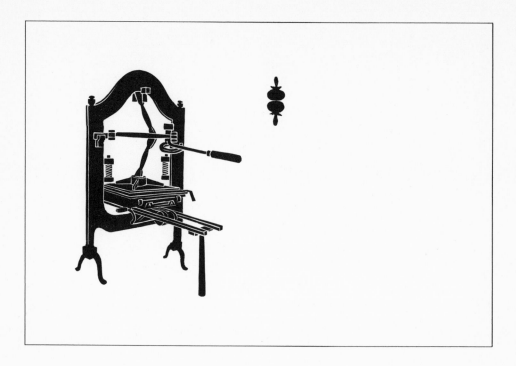

A KEEPSAKE FOR THE TALK BY MR. HERBERT L. BAKER ON RECENT DEVELOPMENTS IN THE MANUFACTURE AND OPERATION OF PRINTING PRESSES, AT THE MEETING OF THE SOCIETY OF PRINTERS ON MARCH 4, 1915

PENSILVANIA

WR

THE *first watermark in paper made in America was the word* COMPANY. *The second device is shown above. The monogram* WR *is on one half of the sheet, and the balance of the watermark on the other half.*

23 THE SECOND AMERICAN WATERMARK, REPRODUCED FOR THE
S. A. KIMBER TALK, APRIL 1915

A KEEPSAKE
FOR THE VISIT OF THE SOCIETY OF PRINTERS TO THE WIDENER LIBRARY OCTOBER FOURTEEN MCMXV

THE HARRY ELKINS WIDENER MEMORIAL LIBRARY : HARVARD UNIVERSITY : CAMBRIDGE

THIS OUR NOBLE ART

¶ And this our noble art of Printing is the very Foster Mother of all Learning; for though the few had Books before Gutenberg gave us our Art, not until Printing came could Learning, yes and Wisdom also, knock at every man's door.

From the Latin of Cardelius. 1546

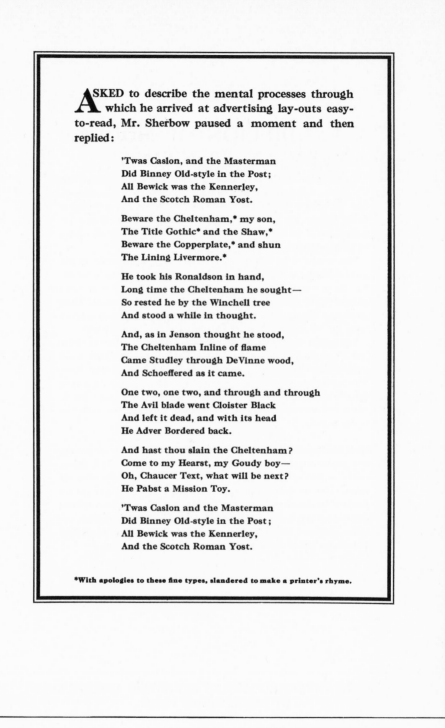

ASKED to describe the mental processes through which he arrived at advertising lay-outs easy-to-read, Mr. Sherbow paused a moment and then replied:

'Twas Caslon, and the Masterman
Did Binney Old-style in the Post;
All Bewick was the Kennerley,
And the Scotch Roman Yost.

Beware the Cheltenham,* my son,
The Title Gothic* and the Shaw,*
Beware the Copperplate,* and shun
The Lining Livermore.*

He took his Ronaldson in hand,
Long time the Cheltenham he sought—
So rested he by the Winchell tree
And stood a while in thought.

And, as in Jenson thought he stood,
The Cheltenham Inline of flame
Came Studley through DeVinne wood,
And Schoeffered as it came.

One two, one two, and through and through
The Avil blade went Cloister Black
And left it dead, and with its head
He Adver Bordered back.

And hast thou slain the Cheltenham?
Come to my Hearst, my Goudy boy—
Oh, Chaucer Text, what will be next?
He Pabst a Mission Toy.

'Twas Caslon and the Masterman
Did Binney Old-style in the Post;
All Bewick was the Kennerley,
And the Scotch Roman Yost.

*With apologies to these fine types, slandered to make a printer's rhyme.

❧ EXHIBITION OF MODERN AMERICAN PRINTING

A N Exhibition of Modern American Printing, to which you are invited to contribute, will be held from November 13 to November 18, 1916, in the Gallery of the Fine Arts Department of the Boston Public Library. The exhibition is under the auspices of the Boston Typothetæ and of the Society of Printers, with the coöperation of the officials of the Boston Public Library.

The purpose of the exhibition is twofold. First, to demonstrate the progress of printing in recent years, so that those not now thoroughly familiar with the best in printing may see what is being done. Second, to provide a stimulus to the interest in printing from an educational standpoint. There are various schools of designing, courses in business administration, advertising and printing classes which will make full use of this exhibition.

The basis of the exhibition is the collection made by the American Institute of Graphic Arts for an exhibition held last spring in New York, which included carefully selected examples from all parts of the United States. To this collection, to demonstrate the standards and resources of the printing industry here, will be added such examples of printing produced in Metropolitan Boston as are chosen by the committee from those offered in response to this invitation.

The exhibition will be widely advertised and will have a large attendance. It is expected that those who visit it will be influenced to use printing to a greater extent, directly to the benefit of those whose work is shown.

The exhibits will be given general or individual descriptive titles, and credits to the printers represented, and will follow the grouping of displays used by the American Institute of Graphic Arts. There will be different classifications for books, catalogues, advertising literature, periodicals, circulars, stationery, etc. Exhibits of individuals or firms will not be grouped as such, but will be distributed under their proper classification.

GIAMBATTISTA
BODONI
OF PARMA

Mr. President and Members of The Society
of Printers:

In selecting, as the subject of your meeting
tonight, Bodoni, the printer of Parma, on
this centennial anniversary of his death, you
have done a very wise and just thing. For
though he may have been over-praised and
honoured in his own day, he has certainly
received rather more than a fair share of
neglect in ours. While I am very sensible
of the honour, I am not so sure of the wisdom of your having asked *me* to talk to you

7

B

A

28 (A) OPENING PAGE OF T. M. CLELAND'S LECTURE ON BODONI (PUBLICATION VIII, P. 74);
(B) AUTOGRAPHS ON A COPY OF THE F. W. GOUDY SOUVENIR FOR DECEMBER 1916 (KEEPSAKE 26; SEE P. 88)

29 MEMENTO OF A CATALOGUE CLINIC HELD FEBRUARY 20, 1917, AND SKETCH BY W. A. DWIGGINS IDENTIFYING PERSONS DEPICTED IN HIS 1917 DRAWING

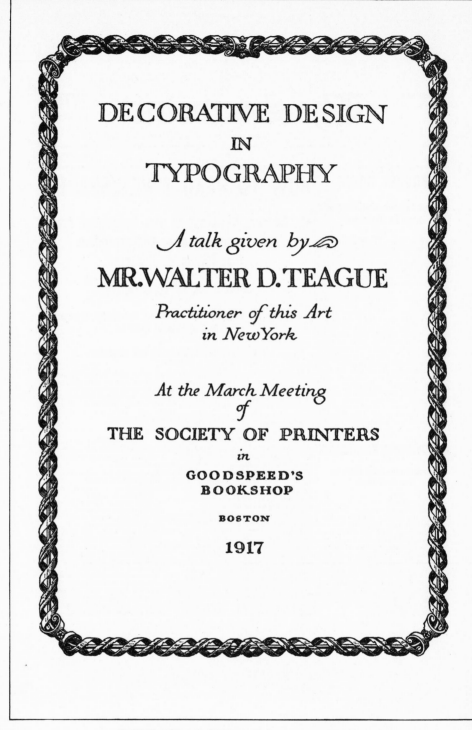

DECORATIVE DESIGN
IN
TYPOGRAPHY

A talk given by ⤙

MR.WALTER D.TEAGUE

Practitioner of this Art
in New York

At the March Meeting
of

THE SOCIETY OF PRINTERS
in

GOODSPEED'S
BOOKSHOP

BOSTON

1917

THE WEATHER
Fair and Warmer

The Souvenir

EXTRA
6.30 O'CLOCK

ISSUED AS A KEEPSAKE OF THE APRIL MEETING OF THE SOCIETY OF PRINTERS

ROOM J   BOSTON, MASS., APRIL 17, 1917   CITY CLUB

BODONI GOING

Reports Indicate that Work Will Soon be Exhausted

BOSTON, April 17—According to President Whitmarsh the demand for copies of T. M. Cleland's work on Giambattista Bodoni, issued in limited edition by the Society of Printers, has nearly depleted the supply on hand.

Orders come in by each day's mail. As the number of copies on hand decreases there seems to be an even greater desire to possess this unique volume.

Many members of the Society have already ordered extra copies for distribution among friends. In addition to this, requests have been received from public libraries, printers' organizations, book lovers, and others,—a condition of which all will be glad to learn.

It is gratifying to note that this first book of the Society has won such marked approval. A suggestion has been made that members aid in further distribution, advising people most likely to be interested as to where the book can be obtained. This plan will no doubt be adopted at once.

A PROVIDENCE PILGRIMAGE

Arrangements Being Made for Trip Next Month

Member Harry Lyman Koopman sends word that he would be delighted to have the Society visit Providence in May. He says there will be one new treasure to show—a very choice Napoleon Collection, not large, but rich. The Annmary Brown Memorial still displays its treasures, and Mr. Foster will be glad to show the St. Bride Collection. The John Carter Brown Library will also throw open its doors, so that the invitation can be said to come from the Providence libraries. It is hoped that a large number will decide to make the trip. The date will be given later.

HOW TO READ A NEWSPAPER

Mr. Edward McKernon of the Associated Press Delivers an Interesting Address before the Society of Printers

ROOM J FILLED TO CAPACITY

Speaker Urges Members to Take Some Newspaper Statements "With a Grain of Salt"

POEM READ APPROPRIATE TO THE OCCASION

BOSTON, April 17—"Think for yourself, and do not let the newspapers do all your thinking," was one of the points brought out by Edward McKernon in an address on "How to Read a Newspaper" before the Society of Printers at the City Club today. The speaker emphasized the importance and the value of newspapers, and the great good being accomplished by them for the betterment of the world. The tremendous responsibility of editors and news gatherers can be comprehended only by those who study the difficulties of their work. The task of separating the wheat from the chaff is one of no small magnitude.

Another thought presented was that care be used in the selection of a paper to go into the home. There are clean, readable sheets—newspapers that the head of the family need have no fear in bringing to the wife and the children —so that the necessity does not exist for allowing any other kind to invade the sacred precincts of the family circle.

Mr. McKernon spoke of the matter of predictions made by the newspapers. If your paper prints a prediction, watch and see if it comes true. The repeated taking up of space in a newspaper to tell of things that are going to happen, and which never do happen, is an indication that no reliance is to be placed on any articles published. A paper must "make good" once in awhile or its reputation is lost.

THE NEWSPAPER

The following excerpt from a poem by J. T. Watson has special reference to the speaker's text.

Newspaper! who has never felt the
   pleasure that it brings?
It always tells us of so many strange
   and wondrous things!
It makes us weep at tales of woe—it
   fills our hearts with mirth—
It tells us of the price of stock—how
   much produce is worth—
And when, and where, and how, and
   why strange things occur on earth.
Has war's loud clarion call'd to arms?
   —has lightning struck a tree?—
Has Seaver broke his leg?—or has
   there been a storm at sea?—
Has the sea-serpent shown his head?
   —a comet's tail been seen?
Or has some heiress with her groom
   run off to Gretna Green?
All this, and many wonders more, you
   from this sheet may glean.

BLOCK PRINTING AND THE GRAPHIC ARTS
A talk by Mr. Vojtěch Preissig, the
director of the Graphic Arts Department at the Wentworth Institute,
before the Society of Printers, at
the Boston City Club, at their meeting on November 19, 1918.

32 KEEPSAKE FOR THE VOJTĚCH PREISSIG MEETING, DESIGNED
IN HIS STYLE BY GEORGE F. TRENHOLM

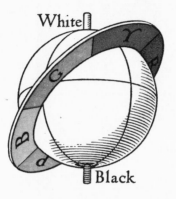

MR. ARTHUR S. ALLEN

Sales Manager of PHILIP RUXTON INC., *New York*

will address a joint meeting of the SOCIETY OF PRINT-
ERS and the BOSTON ARCHITECTURAL CLUB on The
Relation of the Munsell System of Color to Printing
and Advertising, on Tuesday, May 27th.

Mr. Allen has a unique and accurate test to which
he puts numerous color combinations to prove their
color balance. You are cordially asked to bring along
any samples you desire criticized.

The meeting will be held at the BOSTON ARCHI-
TECTURAL CLUB, 16 Somerset Street.

Dinner at 6.30 P. M.

It is important to return the enclosed card, so that
adequate dinner arrangements may be made.

WALTER M. STONE, Secretary
Cambridge 7600

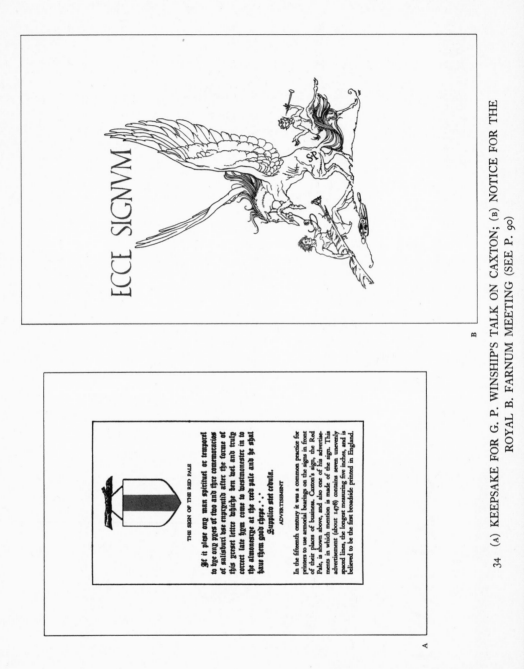

34   (A) KEEPSAKE FOR G. P. WINSHIP'S TALK ON CAXTON; (B) NOTICE FOR THE
       ROYAL B. FARNUM MEETING (SEE P. 90)

THE
CASLON
CROWD

Being a Slight Disquisition, with Exemplifications, on that Typographical Paragon, the Caslon Letter.

Set up for the *Society of Printers* by Carl Purington Rollins. Printed at Yale University Press, New Haven, Connecticut, 1924.

The Caslon Crowd.

Of roman, italic, and title faces there are nearly forty distinct fonts to be had in the best kind, thus permitting a flexibility and unity in type composition impossible with any comparable type face.

Bibliographical Note.

BEING still a willing member of the Caslon Crowd, despite the revivification of Garamond, of Bodoni, and of Baskerville, I am glad to reprint, with a few changes, this bibelot which I issued from the Montague Press in the year 1916.

C.P.R.

The Alphabet in Caslon.

ABCDEFGHIJKLMN
OPQRSTUVWXYZ&
abcdefghijklmnopqr
stuvwxyz1234567890
*ABCDEFGHIJKL
MNOPQRSTUVWX
YZ&*
*abcdefg hijklmnopqrs
tuvwxyz*

35 CARL P. ROLLINS' *THE CASLON CROWD*, DESCRIBED (P. 75) AS PUBLICATION X

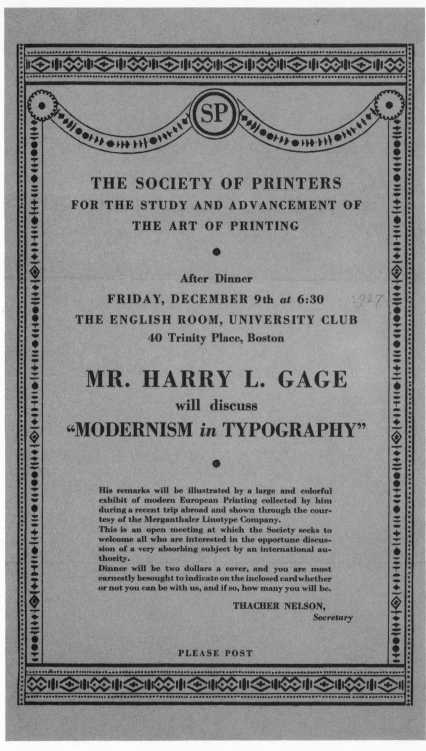

36 HECTIC POSTER FIFTEEN INCHES LONG, ADVERTISING DISCUSSION
OF MODERNISM, 1927

Calligraphy

The Society of Printers: Boston: for the study and advancement of the art of printing, will meet on Tuesday, March 27th, 1928 at the Signet Club, 46 Dunster Street, Cambridge, for a symposium on the subject of Calligraphy Dinner will be at seven; Mssrs. Trenholm, Iorio, Robinson, Harris and Nelson will each say a few words preliminary to a general discussion.

Your presence is eagerly sought, and your kindness in the matter of the inclosed postal much appreciated.

Thacher Nelson, Secretary

MR. L. A. HOLMAN WILL OPEN HIS
PRINT SHOP AT PARK STREET FOR
THE NOVEMBER MEETING OF THE
SOCIETY OF PRINTERS THE TWEN-
TIETH OF THIS MONTH. DINNER AT
THE BOSTON CITY CLUB AT SIX P. M.

MAURICE BLACKMUR, Secretary

THE SOCIETY OF PRINTERS

For the Study
&
Advancement of the
Art of Printing

LIST OF MEMBERS
1930–1931

BOSTON: MDCCCCXXXI

A   B

38 (A) NOTICE OF THE MEETING AT HOLMAN'S PRINT SHOP, NOVEMBER 20, 1930;
(B) OFFICIAL PUBLICATION, NUMBER XI (SEE P. 76)

Thirtieth Annual Meeting

AT THE BOSTON ART CLUB
WEDNESDAY, JUNE 12, 1935
AT 6.30 P. M.

THE Thirtieth Annual Meeting of The Society of Printers will be held on Wednesday, June 12, 1935, at the Boston Art Club, 150 Newbury Street, Boston. Members and their guests are asked to gather at the Art Club for dinner at 6.30 p. m.

A brief business meeting will follow the dinner, when reports of the President and Treasurer will be presented, and officers of the Society and members of the Council will be elected for the ensuing year. The Nominating Committee submits the enclosed list of nominees.

This meeting will mark the recognition by the Society of the distinguished work of our fellow member and former president, Daniel Berkeley Updike. Mr. Lawrence C. Wroth, Librarian of The John Carter Brown Library, Providence, will give a short talk about Mr. Updike and his work, after which we are to view in the Treasure Room of the Boston Public Library the most comprehensive exhibit ever shown of books printed at The Merrymount Press, arranged by Mr. Zoltan Haraszti. A copy of "More Books," the publication of the Public Library, containing Mr. Haraszti's account of Mr. Updike and The Merrymount Press, is being mailed to you.

On this occasion, the Society is assuming part of the cost of the dinner, making the charge to members and their guests only 75 cents. As a large attendance is expected, to assist us in our arrangements, please sign and return the enclosed post card, indicating your intention regarding the meeting.

DANIEL B. BIANCHI
Secretary

HERBERT G. PORTER
President

Panel A

MEETING OF THE SOCIETY OF PRINTERS : BOSTON

"
OLD TIME
WOOD-ENGRAVERS
& THEIR WORK
"

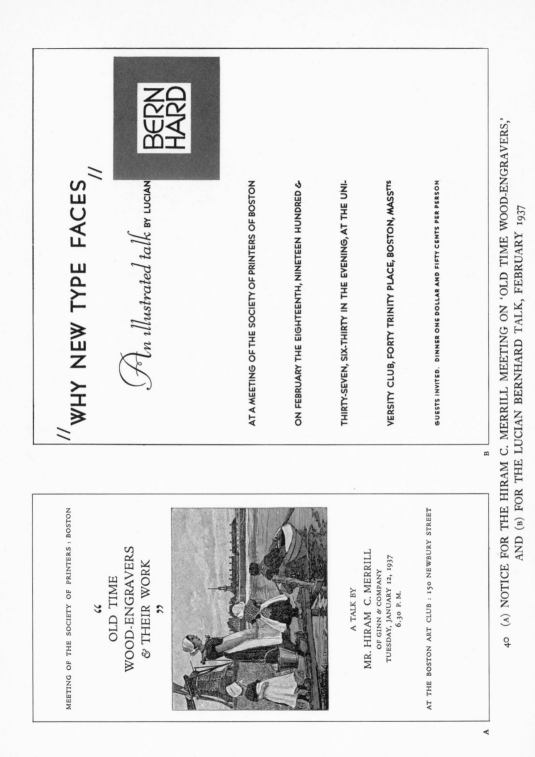

A TALK BY
MR. HIRAM C. MERRILL
OF GINN & COMPANY
TUESDAY, JANUARY 12, 1937
6.30 P. M.

AT THE BOSTON ART CLUB : 150 NEWBURY STREET

A

Panel B

// WHY NEW TYPE FACES //

An illustrated talk BY LUCIAN

BERNHARD

AT A MEETING OF THE SOCIETY OF PRINTERS OF BOSTON

ON FEBRUARY THE EIGHTEENTH, NINETEEN HUNDRED &

THIRTY-SEVEN, SIX-THIRTY IN THE EVENING, AT THE UNI-

VERSITY CLUB, FORTY TRINITY PLACE, BOSTON, MASSᵀˢ

GUESTS INVITED.   DINNER ONE DOLLAR AND FIFTY CENTS PER PERSON

B

40 (A) NOTICE FOR THE HIRAM C. MERRILL MEETING ON 'OLD TIME WOOD-ENGRAVERS,'
AND (B) FOR THE LUCIAN BERNHARD TALK, FEBRUARY 1937

B

TYPES &
TYPE DESIGN
an Illustrated Talk by
FREDERIC W. GOUDY
T.D.P., R.E.*

at a meeting of The Society of Printers of Boston October 21, 1937, at the Boston City Club, Somerset Street. Dinner at 6.30 p.m. One dollar and fifty cents. Guests are invited

*T.D.P.—Type Designer Prolific. R.E.—Raconteur Extraordinary.

A

SOCIETY OF PRINTERS · MAY·20·1937

WE have had a good year—so at the
Annual Meeting and Election of Officers

Let's have a good time. The exuberation on
May 20,'37, at 6.30 p.m.
Boston Art Club

BRING a book, a print or what you will, to talk about—a smile and be on time. You may have your tea, coffee, milk or cocktails at the table and make your own speech instead of listening to one, if you wish. • A member's meeting for "the study and advancement of the art of relaxation." All work and no play makes Jack a dull boy. Let's make it a big meeting!

DANIEL B. BIANCHI
Secretary

---

41 · (A) NOTICE OF THE ANNUAL MEETING, MAY 1937;
(B) KEEPSAKE-ANNOUNCEMENT OF THE GOUDY MEETING, OCTOBER 1937

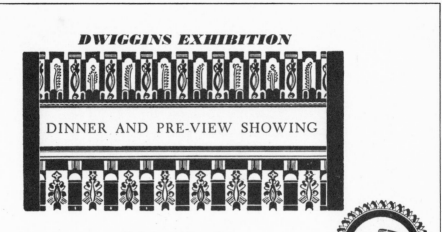

DWIGGINS EXHIBITION

DINNER AND PRE-VIEW SHOWING

On January 25, at 6 p.m.,
the Society of Printers and their guests
will meet for dinner at the University Club,
40 Trinity Place. The speaker of the evening
Mr. Watson M. Gordon, of Doremus & Company, a close personal
friend of Dwiggins, and one who has worked with him over a long
period, will give "An Informal Talk on Bill Dwiggins." The exhibition itself will speak for his art.

After dinner the gathering will adjourn to the Treasure Room of
the Boston Public Library to enjoy privately the most comprehensive showing of Dwiggins' work ever assembled. For the general
public the exhibition will run from January 26 through February 4
from 10 a.m. to 9 p.m.

The officers have been successful in bringing this traveling exhibit
to Boston first. It offers an excellent opportunity for our members to
pay tribute to one of our oldest members and one of America's great
designers. Since we expect a large meeting, will you return the reservation card promptly? While the officials at the Library are graciously holding the Treasure Room open for us until ten o'clock, please
note that the dinner must start promptly at six o'clock.

This exhibit is organized by The American Institute of Graphic Arts

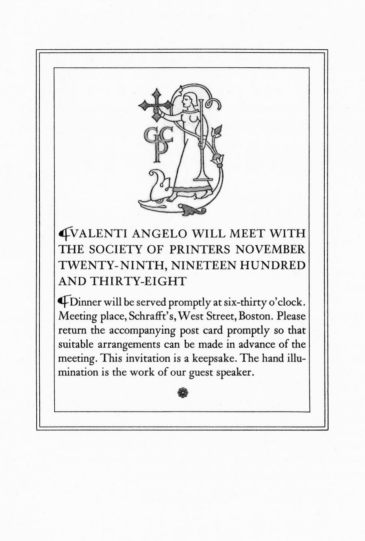

¶VALENTI ANGELO WILL MEET WITH
THE SOCIETY OF PRINTERS NOVEMBER
TWENTY-NINTH, NINETEEN HUNDRED
AND THIRTY-EIGHT

¶Dinner will be served promptly at six-thirty o'clock.
Meeting place, Schrafft's, West Street, Boston. Please
return the accompanying post card promptly so that
suitable arrangements can be made in advance of the
meeting. This invitation is a keepsake. The hand illumination is the work of our guest speaker.

43 KEEPSAKE ANNOUNCEMENT OF THE VALENTI ANGELO
MEETING OF NOVEMBER 1938

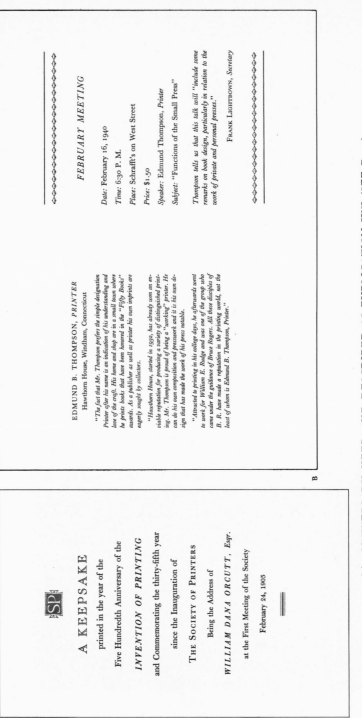

44 (A) ANNIVERSARY *KEEPSAKE*, DESCRIBED AS PUBLICATION XVI (SEE P. 77);
    (B) NOTICE FOR THE EDMUND THOMPSON MEETING IN FEBRUARY 1940

CREATIVE DESIGN

An informal talk by

Dr. WALTER GROPIUS

PROFESSOR OF ARCHITECTURE IN THE GRADUATE SCHOOL OF DESIGN, HARVARD UNIVERSITY, CAMBRIDGE, MASSACHUSETTS

At a meeting of

THE SOCIETY OF PRINTERS

THURSDAY, FEBRUARY 23, 1939, AT SCHRAFFT'S WEST ST., BOSTON, DINNER AT SIX-FIFTEEN P.M. PLEASE NOTE TIME. IN DEFERENCE TO OUR GUEST, DINNER IS EARLY.

GEORGE F. TRENHOLM, *President*
FRANK LIGHTBROWN, *Secretary*

B

SOCIETY *of* PRINTERS: *January 19th*

A

45 (A) ANNOUNCEMENT-KEEPSAKE OF THE TALK BY PHILIP HOFER, JANUARY 1939, AND (B) OF THE FOLLOWING MONTH'S MEETING

A VIEWPOINT ON
TYPE AND ILLUSTRATION

A TALK BY WARREN CHAPPELL

B

Helen Gentry

PRINTER
AND
DESIGNER OF BOOKS

SP

TITTY MOUSE, TATTY MOUSE • DICK WHITTINGTON AND HIS CAT • JACK AND
THE BEANSTALK • THE NIGHT BEFORE CHRISTMAS • COCK ROBIN • OLD WOM-
AN AND HER PIG • PUSS IN BOOTS • TOM OF BEDLAM • TITTY MOUSE, TATTY
MOUSE • DICK WHITTINGTON AND HIS CAT • JACK AND THE BEANSTALK •
THE NIGHT BEFORE CHRISTMAS • COCK ROBIN • OLD WOMAN AND HER PIG

A

46 (A) NOTICE OF THE HELEN GENTRY MEETING, NOVEMBER 1939;
(B) ANNOUNCEMENT OF WARREN CHAPPELL'S TALK WITH HIS ILLUSTRATION

LADIES' NIGHT AND VISIT TO HOUGHTON LIBRARY

BOOKS and manuscripts at Harvard College have long been one of her chief glories. Through the courtesy of Mr. Philip Hofer, Curator of the Graphic Arts at Harvard, the SOCIETY OF PRINTERS, their friends and ladies, have been invited to view these rare treasures in the new Houghton Library, TUESDAY EVENING, MAY 5TH, 1942. Dinner will be served promptly at 6:30 o'clock at the HARVARD FACULTY CLUB, 20 Quincy Street, Cambridge. Dress informal. Automobile parking in rear of Club. You are requested to return the enclosed reservation card at your earliest convenience as the Society must guarantee the number to be served. At 7:45 o'clock the group will journey to the library. Please make a special effort to attend as the committee desires to make this meeting an outstanding social evening. Come at 7:45 if the dinner conflicts with previous plans. A most interesting evening is assured.

CARLTON M. STRONG, *President*   FRANK LIGHTBOWN, *Secretary*

B

January Meeting

will be held at the

SCHRAFFT'S RESTAURANT, 16 West Street
BOSTON, MASSACHUSETTS

on Thursday evening, January 23rd, 1941

Dinner served at 6.30 precisely, $1.50

Guest Speaker, Mr. T. M. CLELAND

THE SOCIETY OF PRINTERS

SP

FRANK LIGHTBOWN
Secretary

CARLTON M. STRONG
President

A

47   (A) T. M. CLELAND'S TALK OF JANUARY 1941 ANNOUNCED WITH A COLORED ILLUSTRATION BY HIM; (B) ANNOUNCEMENT OF LADIES' NIGHT AT HOUGHTON LIBRARY, MAY 1942

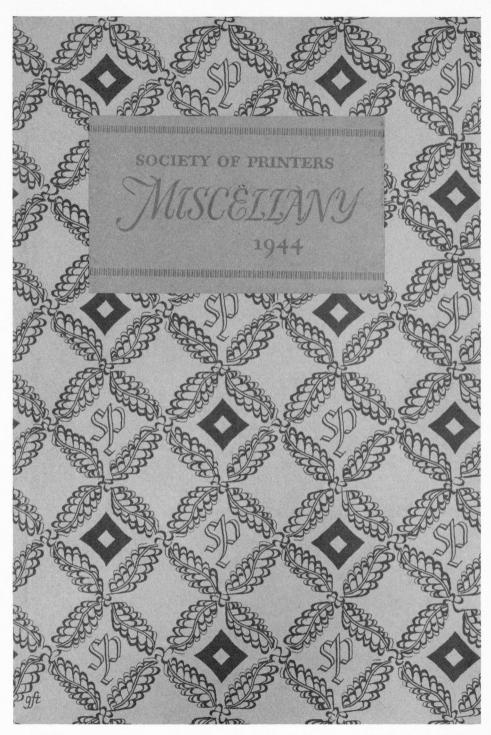

48 COVER OF THE *MISCELLANY*, DESCRIBED AS PUBLICATION XIX (SEE P. 79)

/DAME GREENMANTLE, getting the evening meal ready, begins to speak at dresser, R, crosses to table with bowl of fruit. DAME HOLLAND sitting on a stool in front of fire./

GREENMANTLE: Things have got to a pass where I declare I can't stand any more of it! If somebody doesn't do something soon I declare *I'll* do something! /crosses/ He's been here for *months*, Anna, for *months*!.. the great lummox! /slams down bowl/ There! I've broken it!

HOLLAND: It's a crying shame!

GREENMANTLE: *Everything we've got*'s going down his gullet!—just everything we've *got*! There isn't a *jar* left of the sweets I put away! He skims the milk-pans with his greasy fingers!

(((*3*)))

THE FOUR BELIEFS
BY ROBERT FROST

The Story of T. P. James, who stopped at Brattleboro long enough to be the Spirit Pen of Charles Dickens

THERE was perhaps no better known character than the tramp printer of the early sixties who traveled from town to town, stopping at one place perhaps a week or, if conditions were particularly propitious and the work not too hard, staying for as long as six months. He saw the country, he had no responsibilities, he earned good money which he spent, and while he saved none, perhaps he did not need to, for he could always get a job.

T. P. James was perhaps the best known tramp printer who ever came to Brattleboro, and he stayed here until he became very much more than a local character, for it was he who

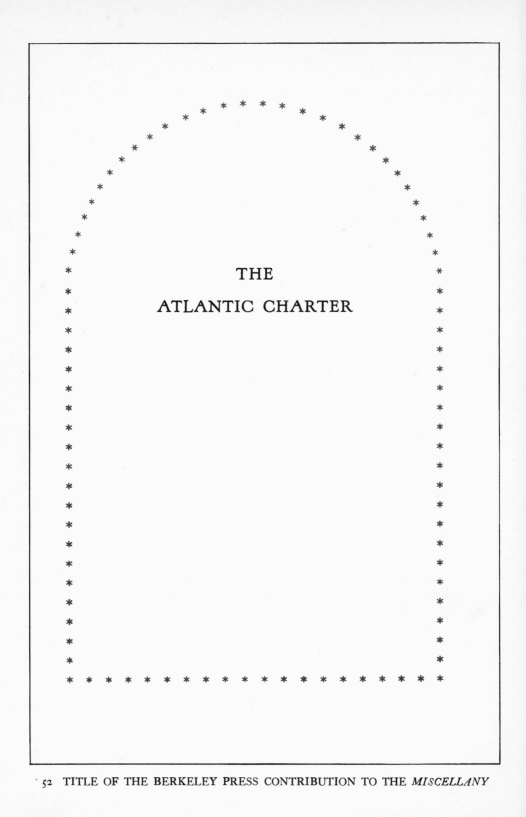

THE
ATLANTIC CHARTER

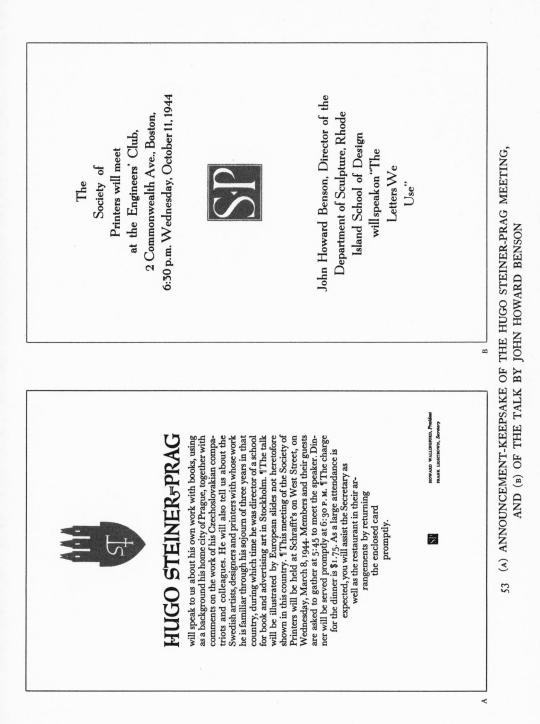

53 (A) ANNOUNCEMENT-KEEPSAKE OF THE HUGO STEINER-PRAG MEETING, AND (B) OF THE TALK BY JOHN HOWARD BENSON

AUTOGRAPHS OF THOSE ATTENDING THE FORTIETH ANNIVERSARY MEETING, MAY 1945

The Society of Printers
will meet at Parker House,
Tremont Street, Boston,
at 5:30 p.m.
on November 10th, 1948

ARNOLD BANK
calligrapher & teacher, will
give an illustrated lecture on
Calligraphy, Lettering &
Type

Cocktail Hour 5:30
Dinner Promptly at 6:30
Lecture at 7:30
at the Chapter Room,
New England Mutual Bldg.

Please note change of date & place of meeting

B

Frederic G. Melcher, of Publishers'
Weekly, will speak before the Society of Printers on January 7th, 1946.

A

55 (A) ANNOUNCEMENT OF THE FREDERIC G. MELCHER MEETING, JANUARY 1946,
AND (B) OF THE LECTURE BY ARNOLD BANK IN NOVEMBER 1948

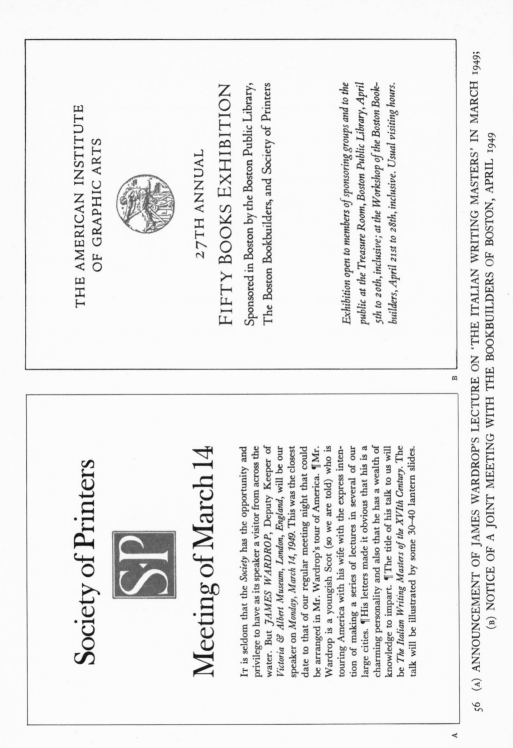

Society of Printers

Meeting of March 14

Iᴛ is seldom that the *Society* has the opportunity and privilege to have as its speaker a visitor from across the water. But *JAMES WARDROP*, Deputy Keeper of *Victoria & Albert Museum, London, England*, will be our speaker on *Monday, March 14, 1949*. This was the closest date to that of our regular meeting night that could be arranged in Mr. Wardrop's tour of America. ¶Mr. Wardrop is a youngish Scot (so we are told) who is touring America with his wife with the express intention of making a series of lectures in several of our large cities. ¶His letters made it obvious that his is a charming personality and also that he has a wealth of knowledge to impart. ¶The title of his talk to us will be *The Italian Writing Masters of the XVIth Century*. The talk will be illustrated by some 30–40 lantern slides.

A

THE AMERICAN INSTITUTE
OF GRAPHIC ARTS

27TH ANNUAL

FIFTY BOOKS EXHIBITION

Sponsored in Boston by the Boston Public Library, The Boston Bookbuilders, and Society of Printers

Exhibition open to members of sponsoring groups and to the public at the Treasure Room, Boston Public Library, April 5th to 20th, inclusive; at the Workshop of the Boston Bookbuilders, April 21st to 28th, inclusive. Usual visiting hours.

B

---

56 (A) ANNOUNCEMENT OF JAMES WARDROP'S LECTURE ON 'THE ITALIAN WRITING MASTERS' IN MARCH 1949;
(B) NOTICE OF A JOINT MEETING WITH THE BOOKBUILDERS OF BOSTON, APRIL 1949

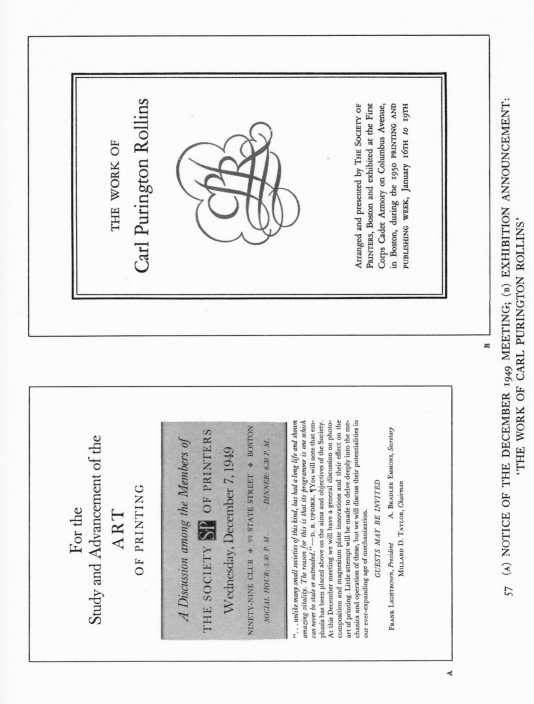

57 (A) NOTICE OF THE DECEMBER 1949 MEETING; (B) EXHIBITION ANNOUNCEMENT: 'THE WORK OF CARL PURINGTON ROLLINS'

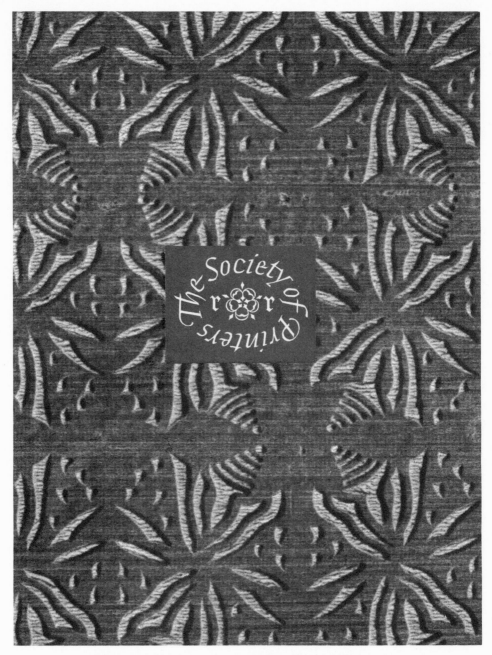

58 COVER FOR THE SOUVENIR MENU OF A DINNER GIVEN TO
RUDOLPH RUZICKA BY THE SOCIETY, JANUARY 1951

THE SOCIETY OF PRINTERS
FOR THE STUDY AND ADVANCEMENT
OF THE ART OF PRINTING

❦

MENU FOR A DINNER
IN HONOR OF RUDOLPH RUZICKA
JANUARY 16, 1951

❦

JOSEPH'S RESTAURANT
279 DARTMOUTH STREET, BOSTON
MASSACHUSETTS

59 TITLE PAGE, IN RUZICKA'S TYPES AND ARRANGEMENT, OF THE SOUVENIR
MENU FOR THE DINNER GIVEN HIM BY THE SOCIETY, JANUARY 1951

There is an Italian proverb: "Print never blushes". I wish I could print what I will attempt to say. I am particularly proud to be honored by the Society of Printers and by the presence of its distinguished guests. The Society of Printers had and has among its members many of my closest friends, not all of them printers. Offhand "printers" seems a loose term for a Society which includes in its membership such a wide range of arts and disciplines. I dare say that the honest-to-God printer-members were always in the minority, yet they are the ones through whose hands the work of all the others must finally pass — they make effective and preserve all our messages.

I have myself no message to deliver to-night, but the sincere wish for the continued advancement of the Society and the arts it represents, in this historically the most articulate of American cities.

R. Ruzicka

60 RESPONSE OF THE GUEST OF HONOR TO THE TOAST 'RUDOLPH RUZICKA'
AT THE DINNER GIVEN HIM BY THE SOCIETY, JANUARY 1951

A

B

(A) MAP FOR THE OCTOBER 1951 MEETING AT THE DWIGGINS STUDIO, HINGHAM; (B) NOTICE OF THE MEETING ON FINE BINDING, DECEMBER 1951

At the December 5th meeting . . . .

THE SOCIETY OF PRINTERS will present FREDERICK W. YOUNG and WALTER F. JOHNSTON of the Harcourt Bindery, who will show their colored film entitled, "Fine Binding." Following the film Miss HANNAH D. FRENCH of the Wellesley College Library will give a short talk on binding of the past.

Social hour at five-thirty   Dinner at six-thirty

Wednesday, December 5, 1951

at the 99 Club, 99 State Street, Boston

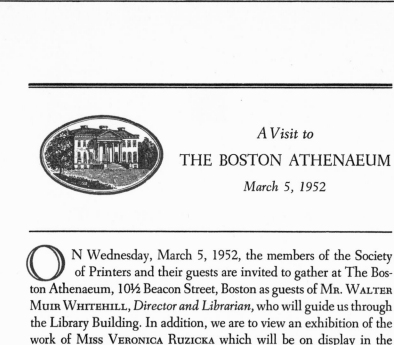

A Visit to

THE BOSTON ATHENAEUM

March 5, 1952

ON Wednesday, March 5, 1952, the members of the Society of Printers and their guests are invited to gather at The Boston Athenaeum, 10½ Beacon Street, Boston as guests of Mr. WALTER MUIR WHITEHILL, *Director and Librarian,* who will guide us through the Library Building. In addition, we are to view an exhibition of the work of MISS VERONICA RUZICKA which will be on display in the Exhibition Room. Due to the early closing of the Athenaeum, we are asked to assemble there promptly at 5.00 p.m. The doors to the building will be locked at 5.30 p.m.

Through the kind invitation of MR. WHITEHILL, we will later repair to the Club of Odd Volumes where supper will be served at 6.45 p.m. After supper, MR. WHITEHILL will speak to us about the Athenaeum Library.

Please return the enclosed post card immediately with your intentions indicated.

MORTON H. BAKER,
Secretary

DANIEL B. BIANCHI,
President

AN INVITATION TO ATTEND

THE BOSTON OPENING OF

THE FIFTY BOOKS

OF THE YEAR

OF THE

AMERICAN INSTITUTE

OF GRAPHIC ARTS

SPONSORED BY

THE SOCIETY OF PRINTERS

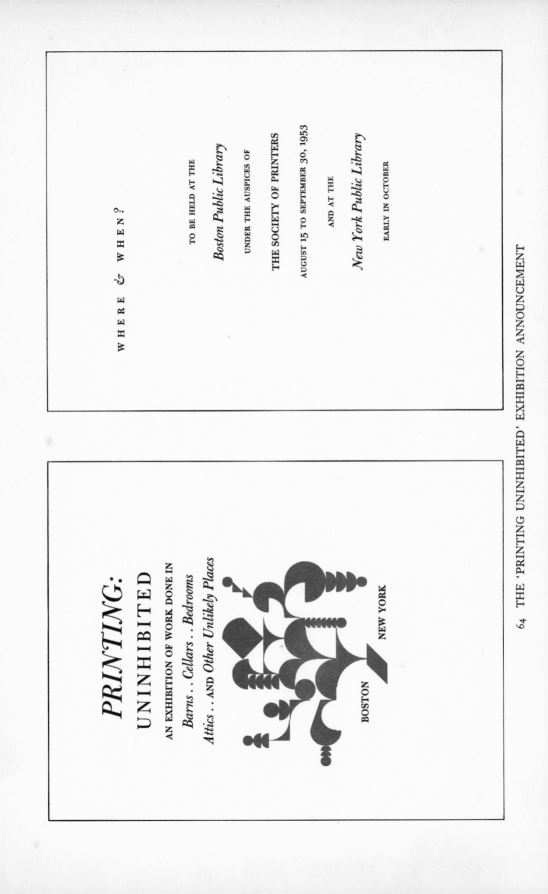